Letter

MW01296385

Welcome, dear reader, to .... issue of your favorite literary journal, *Beatdom*. The theme for this issue is CRIME. It is, of course, a topic pivotal in Beat history, as the artists who were labeled as "Beat" were too often accused being criminals or inspiring criminality, and of course even their writing was often censored due to its allegedly detrimental effect on society. The men and women of the Beat Generation were often fascinated by the criminal underworld, and of course Beat history is marked by a number of crimes, from petty theft to murder.

In this issue we delve into the depths of Beat criminality with an overview by yours truly of the legal troubles faced by the central trio of the Beat Generation – Jack Kerouac, Allen Ginsberg, and William S. Burroughs. Matthew Levi Stevens, an expert on Burroughs, returns to the pages of *Beatdom* to pick up and expand upon this theme with additional details of Burroughs' life in crime.

It's very possible that the Beats would surely have stayed on the straight and narrow if it weren't for the career-criminal and Times Square hustler, Herbert Huncke. Spencer Kansa, a *Beatdom* regular and author of Beatdom Books' first novel, Zoning, recalls an encounter with Huncke in his New York City hotel.

Then we take a slight step outside the Beat realm to look at the mean streets of Los Angeles as seen through the eyes of another mid-20th century author, Raymond Chandler. Chandler's novels were influential on Burroughs, whose pre-cut-up dabblings verged on the hardboiled. Chris Dickerson examines the extent to which Chandler made the streets of Los Angeles his own.

This, our twelfth issue, is yet another star-studded affair, featuring interviews with the Beat legend Amiri Baraka, Kerouac scholar Joyce Johnson, and the one and only Patti Smith. We also bring you a review of Brother-Souls, a biography of John Clellon Holmes by the leading authorities on all things Beat, Ann and Samuel Charters.

In addition, we have an essay by another regular, Chuck Taylor, who questions the quality of Kerouac's poetry, and a newcomer, Philip Rafferty, who asks to what extent the Beat interest in Zen was indeed authentic.

David S. Wills
Founder and Editor-in-Chief

WANTED

For Robbery

Beatdom Issue Twelve
Winter 2012

Publisher
Editor-in-Chief
David S. Wills

Editor
Michael Hendrick

Editor
Katharine Hollister

Cover design: Waylon Bacon
Cover photo Max Kobal/Copyright Zeena Schreck

ARREST AND WIRE AT MY EXPENSE.

TIM DRISCOLL, Sheriff

Silver Bow County BUTTE, MONTANA

WANTED FOR FORGERY

W. H. GEBO Sheriff

Red Lodge, Carbon County, Montana

December 3, 1915.

David S. Wills is the founder and Editor-in-Chief of *Beatdom* magazine. He is also the author of *The Dog Farm*, a novel about expat life in South Korea, and in 2013 his study of William S. Burroughs' relationship to the Church of Scientology will be released. David currently resides in China with his wife and cats. You can read more about him at www.davidswills.com.

Michael Hendrick, Editor, celebrates forty years of publishing poetry with his poem, "Fare Thee Well," in this issue. Recent work in Beatdom includes interviews with Kitty Bruce, Richie Ramone, Hank Williams III, Patti Smith, Ann Charters, and Amiri Baraka. He thinks he is funny.

Kat(e) Hollister: writer, poet, and sometimes player of music. Her writing has been read alongside works by Anne Waldman, and Denise Levertov, for Omaha's *Lit Undressed: Spirit of the Women Beats,* honoring Women's History Month; and several of her poems have received awards and honors. When she is not editing *Beatdom*, she works "in the field," conducting threatened and endangered species surveys.

Spencer Kansa is the author of *Wormwood Star,* a biography of the American artist and occult icon Marjorie Cameron. His debut novel, *Zoning*, was published last year by Beatdom Books. His interviews with William S. Burroughs, Allen Ginsberg, Paul Bowles, and Herbert Huncke feature in Joe Ambrose's book *Chelsea Hotel Manhattan*. He is working on a biography of Zeena Schreck. For more info visit: www.spencerkansa.com.

Zeena Schreck is an artist/photographer, avant-garde musician, author, animal rights activist; yogini in the Drikung, Karma Kagyu and Nyingma Tantric Buddhist lineages; and the spiritual leader of the Sethian Liberation Movement. For more info visit: www.zeena.eu

Chris Dickerson is an award-winning journalist, now novelist, poet, and playwright. His recent novel, *I Only Wanna Be With You*, and his latest book of novellas, *Beyond the Horizon - Hollywood Stories*, are both available on Amazon. He currently lives in Los Angeles. You can learn more about Chris and his upcoming projects on Facebook.

Matthew Levi Stevens is a writer, researcher, and online commentator. He is the author of 'The Magical Universe of William S. Burroughs' and with his partner the artist Emma Doeve recently compiled & edited 'Academy 23' – an 'unofficial' celebration of William S. Burroughs & The Final Academy. For more information see: www.whollybooks.wordpress.com

MCD (Michael CoyoteDog) born in Chicago, has seen his spirit take him many places both inward and outward. Currently he resides in Arizona, spending most of his time in coffee houses wondering why the baristas wear pistols. He has been writing poetry since childhood; is working on his first novel; has a beautiful life, friends, and likes to feed the birds.

Philip Rafferty is a recent graduate from the MA English program at CUNY Brooklyn College. His work "A Play of Force and a Play of Forces" was featured at the Fourth

Annual Brooklyn College Graduate English Conference, his fiction has appeared in *Montage,* and he is the first humanities recipient of the Stony Brook University URECA Creative Research Grant.

Charles Lowe's writing has appeared or is forthcoming in *Essays & Fictions, Guernica, Fiction International, the Pacific Review, Hanging Loose, Midway Journal*, and elsewhere. His fiction has been nominated for the Pushcart Prize. He lives with his wife and daughter in Zhuhai, China, where he is an Associate Professor at United International College.

Catherine Bull is a poet living in Portland, Oregon. She is a graduate of Oberlin College and has a Masters in English/Creative Writing from U.C. Davis, and a dog named after Twyla Tharp. She writes about poetry (and other sorts of books, plus ten-word film reviews) at www.catherinebull.com.

Chuck Taylor operates the annual Beat Art and Literature Festival with Christopher Carmona. The third go will be in Edinburg, Texas. The Beat festival is totally free and all artists are treated as equals. His latest book is a memoir he wrote, he hoped, to make a little money, *The One True Cat*, and that's right, he's made little money.

Jamie McGraw lives in and sometimes leaves North Carolina. She is currently enrolled in Queens University of Charlotte's MFA program. Previous work has been published in APA journal *Families, Systems, and Health,* Red Fez, and r.k.vr.y.

Holly Guran, author of *River Tracks* (Poets Corner Press) and *Mothers' Trails* (Noctiluca Press) is working on a series based on life in the nineteenth century cotton mills. She earned a Massachusetts Cutural Council award (2012), has been a presenter in the Massachusetts Poetry Festival, and is a member of Jamaica Pond Poets. Recent publications include *Slipstream* and *Westchester Review.*

Velourdebeast grew up in Northern California where she was raised by raccoons and fog. When she's not writing, she spends her time foraging for her dinner and napping on broad mossy big leaf maple branches. She wears a dress made out of cormorant feathers, and jewelry made of abalone. She writes stories on paper wasp nests and sends them to Beatdom via a coyote courier.

Alireza Abiz is a Persian poet, literary critic and translator. He has so far published three collections of his poetry in Persian. His poetry has appeared in different anthologies and all major Persian journals and literary websites. Some of his poems have been translated into Arabic, German, and English. He is an award winning translator and has translated some important English and American poets into Persian including William Butler Yeats, Seamus Heaney, Derek Walcot, Allen Ginsberg, Ted Hughes, and Basel Bunting.

Waylon Bacon, cover designer and wondrous artist creates films which have screened regularly at the San Francisco Underground Short Film Festival, the Berkeley Video and Film Festival, and the BCM Horror Film Festival. Additional screenings include Comic Con International Film Festival and the Fright Night Horror Film Festival in Louisville, Kentucky. For more, see www.waylonbacon.com

Somebody Blew Up America:
A Conversation with Amiri Baraka

by Michael Hendrick

Amiri Baraka *IS* Beat.

He walked away from the scene in Greenwich Village, where he edited literary journals *Yugen, Kulchur, and The Floating Bear* from 1958-65. Working with Hettie Cohen, Michael John Fles and Diane Di Prima, respectively, the journals brought new works by new names to the light of day. Featured writers included: Jack Kerouac, William S. Burroughs, Gregory Corso, Allen Ginsberg, Phillip Whalen, and Michael McClure. He co-founded Totem Press and was influential in the launching of Corinth Books. *Yugen* magazine was perhaps most significant for the platform it provided for the 'new' Beat writers, allowing their work to find a place in one of the first venues to give credulity to the movement.

A wise and controversially outspoken man, his views have kept him on the Outside, the Beat side. The U.S. Air Force discharged him after two years of service due to his belief in communism. In 1961 he was arrested for distributing obscenity for mailing copies of *The Floating Bear, Issue Nine,* to subscribers; his presence at the 1967 riots in Newark, New Jersey, saw him arrested and severely beaten by police. It was also the year he changed his name from LeRoi Jones to Amiri Baraka. The charges against him were eventually dropped and much of his support came from the Beat community.

From *Preface to a Twenty Volume Suicide Note*, his first book of poems in 1961, to his upcoming play, *The Most Dangerous Man in America*, he has stayed the course, worked and fought for his belief in an equitable society.

With the death of Reverend Martin Luther King, Jr., (who visited his Newark home a week before his murder), he left the mostly-white Bohemian literary scene and the environs of the East Village to take up a more radical stance towards Black Nationalism. Despite distancing himself from the Beats in the mid-sixties, Baraka read poetry and attended panel discussions at Beat-haven Naropa Institute through the 1980-90s, and remained friends with Ginsberg until Allen's death in 1997.

More recently his poem "Somebody Blew Up America" brought an end to the State of New Jersey's 'Poet Laureate' post when Governor Jim McGreevey took umbrage to the poem's questioning of the events surrounding the 9/11 destruction of the World Trade Centers. The 'Who?' of the exploding owl in the poem echoes the angst of Ginsberg's voice in "Howl." Having heard Ginsberg recite "Howl" live from ten feet away, this writer finds both poems equally as exciting and important.

Baraka has been called 'the triple-threat Beat'; his talent has brought him recognition and awards not just in poetry and prose but also in theater as an Obie Award winning playwright. In addition to his appearances in film, theater and the worlds of poetry and prose, he is regarded as a respected academic, having taught at the State Universities of New York at Stony Brook and Buffalo, Columbia University and other institutions.

A small sampling of the awards bestowed upon him include the PEN Open Book Award, the Langston Hughes Award, the Rockefeller Foundation Award for Drama, and National Endowment for the Arts and Guggenheim Foundation fellowships. Additionally, he is a member of the American Academy of Arts and Letters. Maybe one of the most bittersweet titles placed on him is that of the Poet Laureate of Newark Public Schools, which he received after Gov. McGreevey's actions against him.

We started by asking why he walked away from the Beat Movement, which gave him a vehicle to establish himself as writer/thinker/activist to a wider audience.

~

Well, that whole thing [Beat Movement], was very explosive but remember that the whole Civil Rights Movement was intensifying. I got out of the service in 1957. The Montgomery bus boycott had gone on a couple years before. After they had made them successfully made them integrate those buses, they blew up Doctor King's house. At that point, it really began to be clear this was the kind of struggle that was going on - particularly in the south, at least for me, having been in the service for two years.

7

That was the point that it became clear...until they blew up King's house and he says...you know, the black people showed up at his house with their rifles and said, "What should we do, what should we do, Doctor King?" and he said, "If any blood be shed, let it be ours." So my whole generation reacted negatively to that and said, "No, it won't be like that. If people are going to be shooting, they are going to be shooting back and forth."

Malcolm X appeared at that scene with his whole idea about, you know, "You treat people like they treat you. They treat you with respect, you treat them with respect. They put their hands on you, send them to the cemetery."

So a whole generation of black youth responded to that positively as a sign that Doctor King was indeed a normal man instead of some kind of a saintly non-violent kind of perseverant. During that period, the next years of 1958-1960...In 1959, Fidel Castro led that revolution in Cuba so I went down there the next year, 1960, to Cuba and met Fidel, Ché Guevara and all those people. I also met the black activist from North Carolina, Robert Williams, who was in exile in Cuba because he had really been practicing a kind of a self-defense in North Carolina, a thing that actually ended up with him stopping the [Ku Klux] Klan - removing their hoods...and then he found out it was the State Police! Then they framed him for kidnapping a white couple and he went to Cuba to escape that kind of injustice, so I met him.

Anyway, that was the point - 1960 - when, while I had this kind of awareness of the Civil Rights Movement, I actually became much more directly involved in it. So, about 1965, when Malcolm X was murdered, I felt the best thing to do would be to get out of the Village and move to Harlem. I found that for a lot of black people, that event made us take stock of ourselves and move out of Greenwich Village into Harlem. That was actually the point. I began the Black Arts Repertory Theater Company in 1965 at 130th Street and Lenox Avenue.

Who else was involved in the theater?

Larry Neal, poet, and Askia Touré, poet, those were two of the leading figures. Many people came to Harlem, who were not already in Harlem, because they were attracted to the Black Arts Repertory School that we opened. We would send out trucks into the neighborhood every day...four trucks, one had graphic arts, the other had poetry, the other had music and the other had drama. We did this every day throughout the summer of 1965 so that created a kind of militant venue for Black Arts. They found that was desirable rather than having to submit to the continued racism of Greenwich Village.

The perception is that the Village was not so racist.

At that particular point, a lot of young black people felt it was better to move to Harlem to take an active kind of fighting stance against it, rather than to be isolated in Greenwich Village.

Taking action was better than writing about it or publishing work about it?

Right, absolutely...it was not only about the publishing; it was about actually being an activist in that community and on the street and actually making Black Arts relevant to the movement rather than simply commenting on it.

Do you feel that we are losing ground and giving back too much of what was gained then?

Absolutely! It is like one step forward, two steps back. The whole Obama campaign, the victory...on one hand has brought a kind of very sharp reaction. It is like after the Civil War - once the slaves were so-called 'emancipated', that's when you get the Ku Klux Klan and the black 'codes' and all of that strict re-segregation. Rather than ending slavery you got the whole segregation of the south and the whole dividing of the south into black and white even though they were theoretically free from slavery...but the ex-slaves were plunged into sharecropping and many times they couldn't go anywhere. The white people in the south wouldn't let them go until years after slavery was over. They started going north and west. You can read about that in a book called *The Warmth of Other Suns* by Isabel Wilkerson. She charts that whole immigration out of the south by my people.

The Obama Administration...since the first election, racism feels more prevalent.

It's a stirring reaction to that election. Now we have the Tea Party. The Tea Party is correspondent to the Klan. They appear...the whole takeover of the Congress and the House of Representatives certainly existed because of these kinds of racist reaction - whether Trayvon Martin in the South [Martin was shot in February 2012] or the various kinds of murders out in California. It's a sharp reaction and it shows the reaction is not just against black people but even young white people, like those taken up with the whole Occupy Movement across the country. There is just widespread dissatisfaction in society as it is.

How do you feel about the Occupy Movement?

I think it's a good idea. It is uncertain and uneven but still a good idea and many times there are too many people completely lacking in the experience, in social struggle, or just anarchism, walking around who believe in no kind of government and no kind of organized response but certainly who are opposed to blacks in politics and it is a very ragged kind of result that comes out of that - but still the idea is a good idea and whatever kind of result you can get from that, even though it's going to be much less than it would be if it were organized, you still have to support it.

Part of the reason is that it's like the Sisyphus Syndrome. The only thing that's happening now is that, between the republican force pushing to the right, to restore the kind of republican rule to go to back to Bush, which had been more extreme - what is underneath this is an attempt to erect a kind of corporate dictatorship. Coming out of all these republicans' mouths, especially the Tea Party is the whole question that government is too big, that government is the enemy. The enemy is the lack of development. The fact that poverty still poxes this country and the development is, so far, uneven without a gap between the little six-tenths of one percent of the wealthy and the rest of the people. This has grown bigger and, actually, since Roosevelt and the New Deal we were talking about closing that gap. We talked about creating a much more equitable society. Now even the middle class is feeling the kind of strains that the working class is feeling. So the only thing the republicans have done...I mean, look at the surplus that Clinton had, billions of dollars in surplus, George Bush got rid of it...in the couple of terms that Bush had, he got rid of it a couple of times. He got rid of it.

How? The war, certainly...9/11 was, to me, just a door opening to exploit the Middle East.

10

Like the 2.9 trillion dollars that Rumsfeld announced was missing on the day before 9/11? He claimed they didn't know what they did with it...

Right! They didn't know what they did with it...the people who got it know what they did with it... (laughs).

Can any government be righteous?

I'm a communist. I'm a Marxist. I believe that, ultimately, people will become sophisticated enough to understand that they themselves must rule - not just some little, small elitist group of exploiters. That is what the struggle is for - to see if this society itself becomes equitable. It is going to be hard because we are going to have to go through this period of intensified corporate domination, this last ditch struggle and the fact that it is now a global economy. You see that the struggles on Wall Street have affected the whole world and the only way that they feel they can gain any kind of superiority is war. That's when they can hire more workers. That's when they can fill their coffers and that's exactly what they want to do...war...and that's the only way capitalism can remain balanced on two feet, so to speak, but it will never be secure. That's the problem that the people of the world face, that they have to finally overthrow these governments. They have to overthrow the monopoly of capitalism. That's the task that faces humanity if it is ever to be truly civilized. You can't be civilized with capitalism. It is too elitist. Most people are up against it. Most people cannot ever get a real education. Most of us still live in slums. It is something that is destined to be destroyed that will be very difficult to destroy it in its last days.

Speaking of last days, what do you think of the FEMA camps and the things like the Georgia law that is in Congress to bring back the guillotine?

Are you serious about the guillotine?

Yes, it is a bill in legislature. They say they are running out of the drug to kill people with. You also have the Social Security Administration buying thousands of rounds of ammunition lately and you have to wonder what they need that for.

That's the penalty for moving towards a corporate dictatorship because these people, the republicans and the Tea Party and these people, they're not talking about the government. They're talking about *government*. They are talking about straight-out rule by the rich. It may be a terrifying scenario but that is what is in the works unless the people can find the wherewithal, the understanding and the organization to resist it.

   Even in its ragged state, I would rather have the Occupiers than nothing at all. The problem is that, too often, the people in power are opposed to the Occupiers. That's the problem, most of the people who are in these posts, these small bureaucratic posts, they are even acting against their own interests, not to mention the police and those who are charged with keeping the order - an order that does not even serve them! It's a tragic situation. But I don't know what Social Security would be doing with all those guns. I don't know that.

"Somebody Blew Up America." *You were censored by the New Jersey governor for publishing and performing this poem. The media depicts others who have questioned the events of 9/11 as crazy.*

I understand it, yeah. That's it. You got it. All you have to do is open your mouth, like they say you've got freedom of speech - as long as you don't say anything. The minute you open your mouth, then that's the end of that. Then they attack you. It has certainly happened to me. It happens to all kinds of people... even somebody like Bruce Springsteen,

when he first sang that song about 'fighting the yellow man for the white man'. They silenced him for a few years but he managed to come back. It's that way, if you talk to say anything. There is a long history of that, particularly (for) Afro-Americans, but everybody else, too.

Like that attack on the film industry in the fifties, to remove any taint of the Left from the film industry, the blacklisting of the whole film industry. The whole McCarthyism thing and the fact that, during World War Two the United States' closest allies were Russia and China, but after World War Two our closest allies were suddenly the same people we were fighting, Germany and Japan... figure that out! Then China and Russia became our worst enemies. Why is that? It's because they wanted to cut loose any kind of sign of supporting socialism. Since China and Russia were socialist countries our struggle with these socialist countries, then, was to make sure they were opposed to that (socialism). Finally,

12

Russia succumbed and China has been riddled with imperialist advance. Finally, this corporate America is what dominates and wants to make sure that monopoly capitalism and imperialism outlast anything.

Why do you think people do not pay more attention to this?

The people who could make the most noise about it are afraid they are going to lose their whatever, their positions, afraid they are going to lose what they have. The problem with the great majority of people is that they are not organized and sometimes they don't have the facts so they don't know what is going on. It happens too often, even if you elect good people...like in Newark back in 1970, the first black mayor, the second black mayor. We haven't had a white mayor in Newark since 1970...but then we get somebody like Cory Booker, the present mayor, who actually is sent here by corporate ventures to turn the whole advance, the drive to some kind of equitable city government, around. Now we are struggling against that. Now we have a situation where the mayor is trying to sell our water to private interests. It's unbelievable. He is trying to sell the water plus about two thousand acres of land where we have the water.

Water is getting more expensive, like oil.

That's what they want to do, is jack the prices up and so this is an ongoing struggle. The largest corporation in Newark, which is Prudential Insurance, the largest insurance company in the world, they haven't paid any taxes since 1970. One of their buildings is worth 300 million dollars a year in taxes. They were given a tax abatement in 1970. That was the 'white-mail' they put on the new black city government, "Either give us a tax abatement or we are leaving." That is not supposed to be eternal. I mean, you could give them a thirty-year abatement and it still would be over by 2000. We still have twelve years of twelve times 300 million dollars a year, we wouldn't have a deficit...but they refuse to pay their taxes. They built an arena. They have the NCAA [basketball]; they have the Devils hockey team, which is an interesting idea for Newark. When they have all kinds of big events, they say we owe them money. They utilize our water. They utilize our police for security. We have to pay the police overtime any time they have an event and they say we owe money.

Funny how all the venues are named after financial institutions these days, as opposed to names of great people.

That's right. That's just an indication of where everything is going. Everything is named after a bank or some other kind of corporation...even baseball stadiums. That's absurd. Here everything is named after Prudential. (laughs)

Which medium do you find most useful in reaching people and motivating them?

The problem, again, is the control by the organizations. In the sixties, for instance, the whole emergence of abstraction and the corporations first fought against abstraction.

That is the problem with the arts...it is like "freedom of the press". You can have freedom of the press if you own a press otherwise you have to deal with mimeograph machines and small distribution. That's the way it is with all of the arts. That is the theater of grants. Somebody has to bestow that support upon the artist. Unless you really qualify, philosophically, to be in those venues, you are not going to be there.

I produced a play back in the sixties when I was perhaps unclear what I wanted to say, though they could deal with that to a limited degree. Back then it made it very, very difficult for me to get anything onstage. I have a play coming out in the spring about [W.E.B.] Dubois, called *The Most Dangerous Man in America*. That's what the FBI called him. It'll be a month run at a small theater on the Lower East Side.

You are accomplished and awarded in so many art forms...if you were to be remembered by one piece of work, what would you choose it to be?

I think the book on black music, *Blues People*, that I wrote...people still quote that and cite that. I think that is the most important one. *Blues People* came out in 1963 and is the book of mine that is the most constantly-referenced. I think it was the most popular. I have had other works which had a great deal of *infamy* (laughs) in the United States.

It's about African-American music from Africa and how it developed in the United States. The seeds of that book came to me in a class I had with a man named Sterling Brown, a great poet who was my English teacher at Howard University. A friend of mine named A.B. Spellman who is also in the book, and who wrote a book called *Four Lives in the Bebop Business,* we had both finished class and he invited us to his house because we had some pretensions of knowing about the music. Once we were there, he showed us. He had this library with music, by genre, chronologically, by artist, and he told me, "That's your history."

In that kind of capsule statement what he was saying was that if you analyze the music, if you follow the music, you'll also find out about the peoples' history. So that's what I did – tried to show how when the music changed it signified change in the status of the people and their condition. Everything about their lives has undergone some important change and the music is a result of the affect of the change. It goes to the earliest kind of music - the slave song, the early blues, the city blues, you know, the kinds of variations on that...like coming into the north and how it affected the music. It covers up to the 1960s.

You collaborated with The Roots about ten years ago...in hip-hop. Who are the most important artists or have been?

It changed a great deal from the early hip-hop of the 1970s, which was just a field called 'rap'. Hip-hop is actually a kind of a category that includes different aspects of it all...the DJ, the rapping, graffiti, break dance. Rap, particularly, changed a great deal from the 1970s. The early rappers were much more conscious of making a social statement of protesting the kind of conditions they lived in and that black people lived in. It was really a kind of urban journal type thing, like Afrika Bambaataa from the South Bronx. Then, later on, people like Kurtis Blow and Grandmaster Flash and the Furious Five.

RunDMC was a period of development of that, put together by the guy (named) Russell Simmons, who then became rap's biggest entrepreneur.

Do you think people like Russell Simmons can be as well-accepted and still keep an edge?

People have to sort that out themselves and find out how those kinds of ties (either) support what they are doing or obstruct it. They might just change what they are doing or what they thought and come out with something that may not be as important as what they were doing before. It depends on how you deal with relationships with those institutions and organizations.

Can you tell more about your new play?

The play is about W.E.B. DuBois, when he was about eighty-three years old and was taking a very activist position against nuclear weapons and everything, including going to conferences in Europe to protest nuclear weapons. He was indicted as an 'agent of foreign power', being a 'father' of books. He had just run for political office, he and a man named Vito Marcantonio, a lawyer who was really the last Italian communist in the U.S. Congress. Anyway, when DuBois was indicted because he was in a peace organization [*he was chairman of the Peace Information Center, formed in 1950*], they had the trial in Washington, DC, and Marcantonio defended him. He was the lawyer.

It was a drawn out trial but finally he won the case because it turned out that the chief witness against him was, in fact, the man who had invited DuBois to join the peace organization. So the thing was overthrown but DuBois was prescient enough to understand it, that he said, "Now the little children will no longer see my name."

After that they took his passport and tried to keep him from traveling. Then in 1958, the Supreme Court overthrew that ruling and gave him back his passport so he was able to travel throughout the world...Europe, Russia, China. He had been invited to edit *Encyclopedia Africana* by Kwame Nkruman, who was the newly-elected Prime Minster of Ghana. He went there, declared his membership in the Communist Party and he died in Ghana on the day before the March on Washington, which was started by Reverend Martin Luther King, so it's a real cycle.

That covers a lot of territory.

It is going to be mainly the drama of just before the indictment...and how they prepared for this trial. The main part of the play is the trial, itself, and the rest focuses on his travels around the world, particularly Russia, China and Ghana. That should be out in spring of next year [2013].

Did you have a personal relationship with Malcolm X?

I met Malcolm one time, after he had his house in Long Island firebombed and he was moving around Manhattan. I saw him, actually, with a man named Mohamed Babu at the Waldorf Astoria, where Babu had a room. We met into the wee hours of the morning. That was the only time I actually talked to Malcolm.

You and Lenny Bruce were often mentioned in the same news stories and seem to have been crucified at the same time.

I didn't know him. Like I said, if you speak out and identify with any kind of activism you are going to get jumped. That's it – and you can't expect any other thing to happen.

Did you like his act? Were his racial routines funny to a black person?

Sure, at the time. What was relevant is that he was trying to be for real, to bring some reality to America and make a commentary on America and that was the point. Given the content, he was attacked for profanity and obscenity and all those things.

At that time, I was arrested for sending obscenity through the mail [for] publishing *The Floating Bear.* In one of them I had a play of mine in there or a short story... whatever, and an essay by William Burroughs. [The material deemed obscene consisted of "The Eighth Ditch" an excerpt from his novel, *From the System of Dante's Hell,* and the Burroughs' poem, "Roosevelt after Inauguration"].

This stuff that happened to Lenny Bruce was common, given that situation, because that is when that whole attack was common when you tried to do that – you were met with some kind of withering charges. I defended myself in court

by reading the decision on [*James*] Joyce's *Ulysses* and certainly that won the decision for me... (laughs).

~

The 1934 Supreme Court decision to lift the ban on *Ulysses* opened the doors for the publishing of many literary works besides those published by Baraka. Joyce's book was used in the defense of novels *Lady Chatterley's Lover* and *The Tropic of Cancer*. The works of Amiri Baraka have, similarly, pushed open doors for new generations of creative minds to pass through.

Mr. Baraka was open and generous with his time. He still reads poetry in performance and we encourage you to see him if you ever have a chance. If you want Beat, he is more real than all the recent movies about the 'usual suspects.' He is a living literary icon and his work should be celebrated by all freedom-loving Americans and World Citizens.

Watch for his new play, *The Most Dangerous Man in America*, in spring and pick up a few of his books while you are waiting. He is the real deal and he speaks more sense than any other public figure that comes to mind.

Salute him and enjoy his work!

3000 BEATNI ... **RIOT IN VILLA** ...

...critic, persisted in the view that the book is important ...one wishing to understand the social history of the 18th ...ry. He holds that the book has literary and historical ...t, and that though erotic, it is not pornographic.

...redecessor passed censors

...ther literary witness, Montgomery Hyde, called the book ...nor masterpiece of erotic literature."

...ther book to run the gauntlet of would-be censors in ...da recently was William Burroughs "Naked Lunch."

...e Attorney-General's advisory panel devoted last year. ...s one, that it was not obscene, within the legal defini- ...n the Criminal Code as amended in 1959.

...t definition states that a book shall be deemed obscene ... "dominant characteristic" of it "is undue exploitation of ...r sex and any one or more of the following subjects: ...ty, crime, horror, cruelty and violence."

...at is "undue exploitation of sex"? That is the question, ...the case of "Naked Lunch." literary critics pointed out, ...ook might be considered brutal and disgusting, seen it ...about the fantasies of a narcotics addict.

...passages that might be considered pornographic, they ...are in fact ridiculous. And it was the author's intention ...ridic and to disgust.

...the English-speaking world in recent years, court de- ...have opened the way to the widespread circulation of ...books as Henry Miller's "Tropic of Cancer" and D. H. ...rence's "Lady Chatterley's Lover"

...one result, subject matter and diction that ... ...had been unprintable are no ... ...rs have cashed in on the nov ... ...ch of the staff would shock ... ...eral through much of her life ... ...ney's memoirs are termed ero ... ...e those who have not had their ...

Heir's Pistol Kills His Wi ... He Denies Playing Wm. T ...

Mexico City, Sept. 7 (UP)—William Seward Burroughs, 37, first ad ... ...then denied today that he was playing William ...pretty, young wife during a drinking party last night ...

Police said that Burroughs, a drinking party last night ...promotion of the ... ...shot, ...three shooter, first told them ...that, wanting to show off his ...marksmanship, he placed a ...glass of gin on her head and ...fired, but was so drunk that he ...missed and shot her in the ...forehead and shot her in the ...

Ginsberg Censored

SPOLETO, July (UPI)— ...Police today asked a judge to ...charge beatnik American ...poet, Allen Ginsberg, with ...reading obscene verse at the ...Spoleto Festival.

Composer Giancarlo Menotti, ...festival chief, said lawyers act ...the offended Ginsberg and "no ...serious consequences is expect ...ed." Police filed the complaint ...after detaining three hours with ...Ginsberg at their headquarters.

It has been estimated that 5, ...000 pairs of double-crossed car ...nivinals now used in Maine's ...Mascerated Bay, compared to ...four pairs in 1935.

Beatnik horror
THEIR CULT OF DESPAIR IS
DRIVING THE TEENAGERS

STUDENT IS SILENT ON SLAYING FRIEND

Held Without Bail After He Listens Lackadaisically to Charge in Stabbing Case

Clasping a copy of "A Vision," ...a philosophic work by W. B. Yeats, ...under one arm, Lucien Carr, 19- ...year-old Columbia sophomore, lis- ...tened lackadaisically to the pro- ...ceeding as he was arraigned yes- ...terday morning before Magistrate ...Anna M. Kross in Homicide Cou ...He was held without bai ...hearing on Aug. 29.

The pale, slend ...little interne ...O'Brien, ...charging, ...having i, ...David Ka ...versity, St ...had been fr ...Vincent J. Ma ...that the defend ...say.

HELD FOR HOMICIDE

Witness Held in $5,00 ...Later in the day Jab ...a 23-year-old merchant ...and former Columbia stu ...had been arrested ...night as a material wit ...case, was held in $5,000 ...proceeding in the cha ...Judge John J. Sullivan ...Sessions. ...Mr. Grumet tol ...that after th ...to Kero ...129""

At Chicago Trial
Folk Singer, Poet Not Appreciated By Judge

BY TONY FULLER ...CAGO (UPI)—It was one ...the "Beatles" days so ...the "Chicago ...tellinger ...

Bowing as he made his way to ...the witness stand Defense ...attorney Leonard I. Weinglass ...carried a harmonium under his ...arm and asked the poet—whose ...most famous poem is "Howl"— ...to identify it. ...Ginsberg, too?" ...", an instrument, Ginsb ...sponed said, wittison ...eneered and it ...

Beat Rap Sheet

by David S. Wills

But yet, but yet, woe, woe unto those who think that the Beat Generation means crime, delinquency, immorality, amorality ... woe unto those who attack it on the grounds that they simply don't understand history and the yearning of human souls ... woe in fact unto those who those who make evil movies about the Beat Generation where innocent housewives are raped by beatniks! ... woe unto those who spit on the Beat Generation, the wind'll blow it back. -- Jack Kerouac

The core of the Beat Generation – Jack Kerouac, Allen Ginsberg, and William S. Burroughs – have often been castigated as privileged kids who slummed it for kicks, essentially pretending to join a lower-class in order to gain something to complain about in their writing. Yet at the height of their fame, there were many who considered them a genuine threat to the morality of America's youth.

It is certainly true that Burroughs came from a higher social class, and that all of them were superficially enthralled at times, with the criminal underworld; and each of them gained a criminal record in the course of creating a literary movement that was mired in murder and drug use. Most famously, they explored the seedy Times Square scene, celebrating people like career-criminal, Herbert Huncke. In their books, these people became the downtrodden heroes of the street. Petty crime was celebrated, and drugs venerated as an essential component of being hip and having a good time. As a consequence, the Beats became vilified in the press, and their image forever connected to the criminal.

But they were no angels, that's for sure. Burroughs, the eldest and purportedly the wisest of the Beats, grew up with a sense of alienation and rejection that caused him to seek people with whom he shared something in common. For him, that was an attachment to the criminal underground that he gleaned through reading. Most notably, he took his inspiration from Jack Black's *You Can't Win*, which portrayed a strong set of ethics as existing among criminals, in stark contrast to the morally corrupt code followed by the law.

As a boy his parents had sent him off to the Los Alamos Ranch School, where the spoiled sons of America's elite were toughened up and turned into real men. Burroughs, however, took the chance to experiment with chloral hydrate, a drug which nearly proved fatal, and landed him in hospital. This was also during Prohibition, and he was picked up by the police whilst drunk.

Burroughs' psychiatrist, during his early days in New York, referred to his patient in journals as a "gangsterling," due to the man's seemingly infantile preoccupation with criminals. Burroughs was fantasizing about robbing Turkish baths and armored trucks, with ludicrously devised plans that would never come to pass.

His real entry to the world of crime came through the friend of a boyfriend, who had a gun he wanted to sell. This was also Burroughs' first dabbling in hard drugs; along with the gun, came a large quantity of morphine. Burroughs relished the opportunity to sell these items and make shady acquaintances, although he never did sell the gun, and took most of the morphine himself.

The men to whom Burroughs attempted this first arms deal were Phil White and Herbert Huncke. They were experienced criminals and, as Burroughs had hoped, his entry to the underworld. Through these men, Burroughs also met Vickie Russell, "Little Jack" Melody, and Bill Garver, three more criminals who bore striking resemblances to the sort of characters Burroughs adored from *You Can't Win*.

When Kerouac and Ginsberg met the man who would become their mentor and friend, he charmed and humbled them with gifts of classic literature. He expanded their minds with poetry and literature and philosophy, and he quoted Shakespeare at length. Yet Burroughs was presently more enamored with pulp crime novels. He was greatly taken by Raymond Chandler and

Dashiell Hammett, whose gritty depictions of urban violence meshed with his own observations.

Like Burroughs, Kerouac and Ginsberg were looking for experiences that they would not find in their coursework at Columbia University. They wanted their minds opened, and in addition to the books Burroughs bestowed upon them, they soon found themselves sampling various illegal substances, and hanging around with criminal types like Huncke. They never delved as deeply as Burroughs, but nonetheless the experiences were formative.

Perhaps the biggest crime in Beat history, and certainly the best documented, was the murder of David Kammerer by Lucien Carr. Carr was a precocious and obnoxious student. He had known Burroughs in Chicago and became friends with Ginsberg in New York. Kammerer, a much older man, whom Burroughs knew from St. Louis, had an infatuation for Carr that caused him to follow the young man around America. It all ended with Carr stabbing Kammerer in self-defense and rolling his body into the Hudson River.

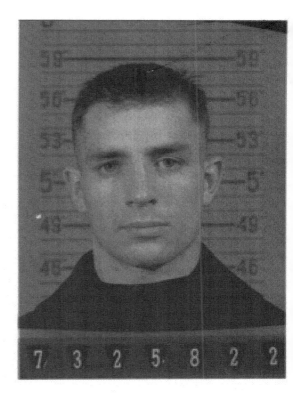

Carr ran to Burroughs for help, and Burroughs told his friend to turn himself in with the support of a good lawyer. Carr then went to Kerouac, who helped him dispose of the remaining evidence. For their troubles, both Kerouac and Burroughs were arrested when Carr eventually followed Burroughs' advice and turned himself in. Burroughs' parents, in what was becoming quite a predictable pattern, came to bail him out, while Kerouac languished in jail, having a somewhat less wealthy and forgiving family.

Despite Carr's protestations, the event was documented or at least referenced throughout Beat history. Most memorably, it was the subject of Kerouac and Burroughs' chapter-by-chapter collaborative effort, *And the Hippos Were Boiled in their Tanks*. In Burroughs' chapters, the influence of his crime fiction reading is far more apparent than elsewhere in his oeuvre.

DENVER
26362
7-11 44

Burroughs was spiraling into the criminal world. With Phil White he was robbing drunks on the subway who sometimes woke and turned violent. Eventually White was sent down for killing a man with Burroughs' gun. Fortunately, as it turned out, Burroughs was picked up for forging a prescription, and the judge sent him home to St. Louis, where his parents attempted to keep him out of trouble.

With Burroughs' departure, the group was falling apart. Critical female Beat, Joan Vollmer, broke down from amphetamine abuse and was taken to Bellevue Mental Hospital, Huncke was arrested for possession and went to prison, and Ginsberg escaped back to his father's house. Then the arrival of another career criminal came, one who would take Huncke's place as inspiration to the Beats: Neal Cassady. Besides, between stints in prison, Huncke's selfish and compulsive criminality was wearing on the patience of everyone, including Ginsberg, whose things he stole and pawned.

Cassady grew up on the streets of Denver. The legends around him are myriad, thanks to Kerouac's mythologizing, but he appears to have been a legendary car thief and womanizer, who knew how to have a good time. He was first picked up by the police at seven, stole his first car at fourteen, and did six stretches in prison for auto theft by the time he appeared on the Beat scene.

Back in St. Louis, Burroughs met his old friend, Kells Elvins, and together they moved to Texas as farmers. Burroughs attempted to grow opium and marijuana with limited success. He moved from South Texas to East Texas to Louisiana, always in search of the freedom of the frontier, but he never found it. Instead, he was arrested for fornicating by the side of the road, and picked up for riding in a car with a known junky. The police raided his home and found his letters to Ginsberg, containing numerous references to drugs. He was looking at several years in the notorious Angola Prison, so he skipped the border and settled in Mexico City, where the next big Beat crime would occur.

At this time, Ginsberg's New York apartment was being used by Huncke and Vickie Russell to store stolen goods. Ginsberg became understandably paranoid that the police would raid his apartment, and wanted the goods out. Carr was also furious that his name was included in letters between Ginsberg and Burroughs, as he was now out of prison for the Kammerer murder, and eager to keep his name clean. These letters also contained incriminating references to homosexuality, and so Ginsberg wanted to be rid of them, too.

When Ginsberg enlisted the help of Russell's boyfriend, Melody, to help move the stolen goods and letters from his apartment, Jack appeared in a stolen car. They loaded it up and headed out, but soon after they were pulled over for making an illegal turn and a high-speed chase occurred. Ginsberg escaped but his letters led the police right to his door, and he was locked up until his father bailed him out.

In Mexico City, Burroughs railed against the tyranny of the American government, and praised the freedom that came with living in Mexico, where the police would leave you alone, and if they did have cause to pick you up, they could easily be bribed. Here he wrote *Junky*, his first novel. It loosely fictionalized his life as a criminal, from his childhood obsession to his life as an addict.

It was there in 1951 he shot Joan Vollmer, now his common law wife, above the Bounty bar whilst attempting to sell a handgun. Although details have always been disputed, it appears they were playing a game of William Tell and the bullet flew too low. Burroughs spent thirteen days in jail before his brother arrived and bailed him out. His lawyer managed to bribe the ballistics expert and the witnesses, friends of Burroughs, corroborated his story that it was an accidental discharge. Burroughs was sentenced to probation, which meant checking in at the police station once a week. Instead, he fled to Europe and ended up in Tangier, where he was once again on heroin, and thankful for the lack of police intervention in his life.

The year 1951 also saw the completion of Kerouac's *On the Road*, a chronicle of his travels across America and into Mexico. The book was not published for another six years, when Viking Press released it in 1957, and the Beat Generation exploded into infamy.

Public sentiment towards those who now became known as "Beatniks" turned decidedly sour. Kerouac's use of pseudonyms caused him a spot of trouble, but most of it fell on the head of Neal Cassady, whose sudden fame as Dean Moriarty resulted in his 1958 arrest for marijuana possession. He was sentenced to five years in San Quentin.

Two years earlier, Ginsberg had read his seminal poem, "Howl," and electrified the poetry community. It was picked up in the same year by Lawrence Ferlinghetti for City Lights Books,' Pocket Poets Series. In 1957, the same year *On the Road* sparked a backlash against the Beat youth of America, Shigeyoshi Murao, legendary manager of City Lights, was arrested; more than five hundred copies of *Howl and Other Poems* were impounded on their way from London. An obscenity trial ensued, and the poem was judged "not obscene."

Shortly after, Ginsberg shocked the literary community by abandoning San Francisco and moving to Paris, to take residence in what became known as the Beat Hotel. Soon he was living with Burroughs and Gregory Corso, and numerous other artists and writers. It was here that Burroughs' classic, *Naked Lunch*, was edited and published, having been written mostly in Tangiers. Published in 1959, the book made its way to the United States slowly, relying on word of mouth publicity. By 1962 it was banned, resulting in the second Beat obscenity trial. This time, however, it took significantly longer to convince the judge of its merit, and it was only in 1966 that *Naked Lunch* could legally be sold in the U.S.

By now the youthful exuberance of the Beats had waned as Burroughs, Ginsberg, and Kerouac mellowed with age. Ginsberg's championing of various freedoms and support for protests throughout the sixties caused him to continually come face-to-face with the police in America and other countries. In 1965 he was deported from both Cuba and Czechoslovakia because of his homosexuality and perceived trouble-making. After the publication of *On the Road*, Kerouac became closer to his mother and spent much of his time at home, more or less out of trouble. Even Burroughs, the most criminally-inclined of the Beats, more or less kept out of trouble for his remaining years. He had always sought his own space in life away from the control of police and the government, and aside from continual searches at the airport, he was largely able to avoid the law.

*

Image notes: The picture of Kerouac is in fact from his entrance to the U.S. Navy. The Cassady picture, however, is an authentic jailhouse mugshot. The collage preceding the article was compiled by David S. Wills and is taken from scans and reproductions of the original news items.

Coming Soon from Beatdom Books

Between 1959 and 1968, William S. Burroughs
actively practiced the methods advocated by the
Church of Scientology. These had a tremendous
impact on his life and work, and featured heavily
in his novels from the 1960s. After attaining a
high rank within the Church in 1968, Burroughs
parted acrimoniously with the organization and
went on to become one of its most outspoken
critics. Consequently, subsequent works about
his life and literature have overlooked the
importance played by the cult, which was an
obsession for him during him most productive and
inventive years.

David S. Wills, founder of Beatdom, has
attempted to set the record straight in
Scientologist! William S. Burroughs and the
'Weird Cult'. Available Spring, 2013.

Bill and Joan. Joan and
Bill. A crime committed with slivers of
mercy, by a man who, when pursued,
      fled. Whose love for Joan was raw,
like a garbage disposal's love
      for shreds of ham, lettuce,
          fingers.

Aching for cash, Bill thrust his collection of
handguns into a bag, set
      to sell the things to any
eager party. The act seemed wrong,
like packing socks into a
      freezer or devouring songs with a
          fork.

      A sale was to take place
above Bounty Bar, in the company of friends
and Joan. Biding time, she swigged gin
      and *limonada*. Biding time, Bill teased,
"Put that glass on your head,
      Joanie. Let me show the boys
          what a great shot old Bill is."

And so, for William Tell, Joan obliged and placed
the tumbler on her head, a hat fit for a fool. A smile, then:
      "I can't watch this, Bill. You know I can't
      stand the sight of blood."

And so, no one watched old Bill fire
the worst shot he would ever fire, the worst shot
no one would ever see.
      A choke, then:
      he considered her temple,
          the wailing hole.

      That night, he dreamed of Joan
looming over him, her lips caked with
ectoplasm, eyes submerged in red.
      A sigh, then: "William,
I've yet to meet a friend, but I think
      God is this faint hum
          in my ear."

Rambo's Bohemia
by Catherine Bull

And so I left, my fists tearing new pockets
in a coat made of bullet holes.
The sweaty blue sky ordered me to dream
and I asked how high!

In ripped fatigues, Appleseed, John J. –
I scattered handfuls of blood
no matter where I tried to go. Homeless most nights
I watched my stars slide across the whetstone sky.

On heavy evenings the rain fell
ringing like spent shells in the heat,
a lullaby I swallowed.

And there, in the midst of expendable shadows,
like bow strings I'd pluck the laces
of my scarred boots, my foot pointed towards my heart.

"To live outside the law you must be honest..."
(Some thoughts on William S. Burroughs, The Beats, & Crime)

By Matthew Levi Stevens

"The Romantic artist is both hero and criminal." – Camille Paglia, on Samuel Taylor Coleridge's *Kubla Khan*

On reading Camille Paglia's excellent collection of articles on poetry, *Break Blow Burn,* I was immediately struck by how many of her statements regarding the Romantics could just as well be applied to the Beats, who of course included the former movement among their influences and inspirations. In common with the Romantics, the Beats surrendered themselves to intense emotion and extreme experience, and certainly made themselves the subject of their art. They would also seek to redefine every aspect of life and how to live it, cherishing friendship and the freedom of both physical and mental exploration, and experimenting with art, consciousness, love, and morality regardless of the conventions of mainstream society. I was also struck by the particular quote above, which has a kind of resonance with another statement I had come across, made by the painter Brion Gysin at the time of his appearance at *The Final Academy* in London in 1982, alongside his long-term collaborator and friend William S. Burroughs, that, "Magic, like Art, is outside the Law."

In many ways the birth of the literary and counter-cultural movement that is the Beat Generation was steeped in an atmosphere of crime. The very name "Beat," as first defined by Jack Kerouac in conversation with John Clellon Holmes, derives from Herbert Huncke: drug addict, jailbird, male prostitute, and petty thief. Also a raconteur and story-teller *par excellence*, he has been famously described as their Virgil in the Underworld of Times Square. He used the expression he had picked up from jazz musicians and hustlers, "beat," (as in "Man, I'm beat") to mean down and out, poor or exhausted – although the never-quite-fully-lapsed Catholic Kerouac would play on the term to imply "beatific" and also the jazz-influenced "on the beat."

Even at the beginning, the origins of what would become Beat Generation is overshadowed by the criminal: all of the key players were enthusiastic experimenters with a wide range of mind-altering drugs, from drug-store Benzedrine to marijuana, and later hard drugs like morphine and psychedelics such as peyote. Burroughs and Huncke were the long-term junkies of the Beat scene, but Ginsberg and Kerouac occasionally shot up morphine with them (even if they didn't use enough or often enough to get hooked – unlike Gregory Corso, who would later start shooting heroin with Burroughs at The Beat Hotel in Paris, leading to a lifelong struggle with addiction), and all of this at a time when "It was just about illegal to talk about dope," as Allen Ginsberg claimed in the Introduction he wrote for *Junky*:

> "There was at the time – not unknown to the present with its leftover vibrations of police state paranoia cultivated by Narcotics Bureau – a very heavy implicit thought-form, or assumption: that if you talked aloud about 'tea' (much less Junk) on the bus or subway, you might be arrested – even if you were only discussing a change in the law."

Of course, in America of the 1940s and 1950s homosexuality was not only illegal but likewise pretty much unthinkable where most decent citizens were concerned, yet one of the things that immediately set the Beats apart was their general acceptance of a more varied sexuality. Burroughs, Ginsberg, and Huncke were all pretty open about their preferences, and although Jack Kerouac and his macho idol Neal Cassady both identified primarily as heterosexual, they had engaged in same-sex encounters and were accepting of the homosexual orientation of their friends. In this light it is an even more tragic irony that one of the key events at the beginning of the Beat legend is Lucien Carr's stabbing of Dave Kammerer because he felt overwhelmed by the older man's obsessive advances, and in a drunken row killed his former friend in what he claimed was "self-defense." In the aftermath of the crime the older, perhaps more worldly Burroughs (who was Kammerer's friend from back in St. Louis, and perhaps could also have been expected to feel a certain sympathy as an older homosexual man rejected by a younger love object) advised Carr to turn himself in at once and plead defense of his honor. Ironically, Kerouac helped Carr dispose of the murder weapon and then took him out drinking and to the movies, and ended up being arrested as an accessory after the fact. When Kerouac's indignant father refused to post bail, he offered to marry Edie Parker if she would get him out. Burroughs and Kerouac then briefly collaborated in an attempt to write up the Carr-Kammerer case as *And The Hippos Were Boiled In Their Tanks*, although it was never published in their lifetimes, and Kerouac would also write about it in *Vanity of Duluoz*.

Later, Ginsberg allowed Herbert Huncke to move in with him (despite stern warnings from Burroughs), and his apartment quickly became a shooting gallery and hock-shop for stolen goods. After being caught in a stolen car, rather than jail-time he was sent for compulsory psychiatric evaluation to determine why a bright student from a nice middle-class family was hanging around with a bunch of degenerate junkies and petty criminals. In another one of the strange links in the chain that comprises the Beat Legend, while Ginsberg is in hospital he met and befriended Carl Solomon, a young writer much enamored of Dada and Surrealism, who would be subjected to shock treatment for depression. Solomon's uncle was the publisher A. A. Wyn, and his friendship with Ginsberg led to the publication of Burroughs' first novel, *Junky*. In recognition of their friendship and asylum camaraderie, Ginsberg later immortalized Carl Solomon in his breakthrough epic, *Howl*.

Junky was a difficult enough book to get published at the time - even with all the alterations and cuts and editor's notes (in parentheses) disputing the author's claims as being at variance with "recognized medical authority" - but the intended sequel, *Queer,* was unthinkable: Solomon warned Burroughs in no uncertain terms that they would both go to jail if he tried to publish such a book. The irony was that as he wrote his second volume of thinly veiled confessional autobiography, Burroughs had very recently seen the inside of a jail, and had only narrowly avoided what could have been a lengthy sentence for murder. Tied with the Carr-Kammerer incident, the most famous death to strike at the heart of the original Beat circle – and one that was to have even greater literary consequence, at least as far as the making of Burroughs the Writer is concerned – was the now infamous shooting of his common-law wife, Joan Vollmer, in Mexico City, when their so-called "William Tell act" went horribly wrong in what Burroughs himself would later describe to me as "just an unforgiveable piece of total... drunken... insanity."

In the Preface to *Queer*, which Burroughs wrote on the occasion of its eventual publication in 1985, he stated:

> "I live with the constant threat of possession, and a constant need to escape from possession, from Control. So the death of Joan brought me in contact with the invader, the Ugly Spirit, and maneuvered me into a lifelong struggle, in which I have had no choice except to write my way out."

But the simple truth is that he had always been a scribe: in numerous articles and interviews he describes at length his literary efforts from childhood, and the image of a somewhat precocious, bookish, and physically awkward young writer in the making, that was as hopelessly Romantic as it was colored by a flouting of moral convention:

> "As a young child I wanted to be a writer because writers were rich and famous. They lounged around Singapore and Rangoon smoking opium in a yellow pongee silk suit. They sniffed cocaine in Mayfair and they penetrated forbidden swamps with a faithful native boy and lived in the native quarter of Tangier smoking hashish and languidly caressing a pet gazelle."

Indeed, Burroughs' descriptions of his early literary efforts abound with sketches of contract killings, dope peddlers, gangsters, and heists – his imagination doubtless fed by reading the likes of *The Wild Party*, a hardboiled jazz age epic poem by Joseph Moncure March, of which he later remarked "It's the book that made me want to be a writer." However, despite this statement, the work that undoubtedly had the greatest impact on the young Burroughs was without question *You Can't Win* by Jack Black. Originally published in 1926, and read by Burroughs in his mid-teens (his account varies as to whether he was thirteen, fourteen, or fifteen), this true life confessional written by a former cat burglar about his life on the road amongst "bindle stiffs, hobo jungles, and rod-riding pete men" not only provided Burroughs with an alternative moral code, but also a source of characters, images, and references (such as the unforgettable "Salt Chunk Mary") that would occur again and again throughout almost all of his writings.

In a world that seemed caught between the end of the Wild West and the rise of the Gangster era, but capturing all of their respective senses of frontier freedom and outlaw glamour, Black explained the concept of the Johnson code: good bums and crooks, who managed to live outside of society and its laws by a kind of "honor among thieves." A Johnson may be a burglar, junkie, pickpocket, or riverboat gambler – but he is still a good man to do business with, and whose word is good. Perhaps more significant still, a Johnson minds his own business and is uninterested in the personal morality of others – but will not stand by if someone is in danger or needs help. To the young Billy Burroughs this must have been a breath of fresh air after the double standards, hypocrisy, and stuffy manners of the St. Louis society into which he had been born. Burroughs' first biographer, Ted Morgan, suggested in *Literary Outlaw* that it was his sense of not belonging, of already feeling an outsider, which caused young Billy to identify with the colorful turn-of-century cast of con-men, drifters, and grifters:

> "In his search for a viable identity, Burroughs deliberately sought out a criminal life. A community of outlaws, such as he had read about in Jack Black's *You Can't Win*, was perhaps the only place a misfit such as he could belong."

This was the world he would eventually encounter in New York after the War. When he first met the "hard-working thief" from the shipyard referred to as "Norton" in *Junky,* who asked him if he knew anybody who wanted to buy a Tommy Gun and some morphine syrettes, Burroughs saw his chance for an entrée into the criminal underworld. It was Bill's desire to belong to this outlaw fraternity that would lead him to the likes of Phil White and Herbert Huncke, and to his first foray into hard drugs. In turn, it was eventually his attempts to set down some of his experiences as an addict that led to *Junky*, his first completed book. In many respects his first attempts at literature were born from experiences steeped in criminality. In this light, his seemingly quite casual decision to keep back some of the morphine syrettes and try junk for himself – despite the warning from Phil White ("Ray" in the story) that "It's bad stuff. The worst thing that can happen to a man." – can almost be read as a self-elected rite-of-passage into the community of outlaws straight out of his boyhood fantasies of *You Can't Win*.

From the hapless attempts to grow and sell weed, to the more serious pushing of junk and "working the hole with the sailor" (robbing passed-out drunks on the underground train with career criminal, Phil White) the life of the junkie is described with unflinching honesty, including the ever-present risk of arrest or OD and the fear of being unable to score and going through a brutal withdrawal. Burroughs would mine his experiences as an addict for many years to come, and indeed what is still considered his masterpiece, *Naked Lunch,* simply could not have been written without it.

Despite the importance of the junk experience to his work, he also stated numerous times that it is unlikely he would ever have written at all if he had not finally come off drugs by undergoing the experimental "apomorphine treatment" pioneered by Dr. John Yerbury Dent of London. Burroughs was convinced that apomorphine was some sort of "metabolic regulator" that reset a patient's metabolism entirely, removing the need for drugs, and he was to champion the cause of this proposed treatment with considerable zeal for some years to come – even utilizing the notion in his literary works as a kind of counter to his metaphor of junk as a model of Control.

That Burroughs the junkie had only emerged from a lengthy period (the figure given was usually "about fifteen years") of near terminal addiction to become William S. Burroughs the Writer, who had infamously been to Hell but was able to come back and tell what he saw like some Post-Modern Ancient Mariner thanks to the miracle of apomorphine, was said so often that in the end it became almost a kind of official line. Throughout the 1960s and 70s interviews and magazine articles would repeat this, and even ask Burroughs about his current attitudes and drug use: while he nearly always spoke positively about cannabis, he usually admitted to little more than social drinking and gave every indication that, other than as subject matter for his writing, hard drugs were very definitely a thing of the past. While this may have been true for a short time – and clearly Burroughs could simply not have produced the substantial body of work that he did if he had continued to be strung out – as the 1970s gave way to the 1980s, it became a less convincing pose, and although most critics, fans, and the general public were still treated to the same refrain, those in the know or who came close to Burroughs' personal orbit saw that something was going on.

The truth is that sometime in the late 1970s, living at the infamous Bunker on New York's Bowery, William Burroughs began fooling around with junk again and inevitably became re-addicted. A number of contributing factors can be considered, and have even been proffered as explanations of a sort: that New York City at the time was awash with what has been described as a veritable tsunami of good quality, reasonably priced smack, that the New York Punk culture, which had adopted Burroughs as its totem "Beat Godfather" enthusiastically mixed chemically-assisted hedonism and drug-fuelled nihilism, that the stream of fans and well-wishers who began to make the counter-cultural pilgrimage to the Bunker would bring offerings, only too happy (as Burroughs' Personal Assistant James Grauerholz would later put it) to "get high with the Pope of Dope," or that the steady decline of his son, Billy Jr., as a result of his own life of alcohol and drug abuse, and the unbridgeable emotional distance between them, was more than the usually cool and detached Burroughs could bear.

Perhaps it was all of these, or none of these. Burroughs himself has said on a number of occasions that asking why somebody becomes an addict is about as much use as asking why somebody catches malaria, the implication being that it is simply "a disease of exposure." Whatever the reason, by the late seventies Burroughs had become re-addicted, and his needs could be taken care of pretty easily in New York. There were always younger friends, like the writer Stewart Meyer, who were prepared to take care of actually copping the dope, an increasingly risky proposition for Burroughs as a man in his sixties, despite blackjack, pepper-spray, and swordstick that he carried. Elsewhere it would be a major logistical problem. Around this time, Burroughs' newfound career as Spoken Word performer was being managed by James Grauerholz to bring in some much-needed money for the aging writer. Although rewarding, both financially and in terms of recognition and reaching out to a new audience, going on tour meant going away from easy access to the street supplies of home.

At this juncture I will declare a special interest, inasmuch as I met William S. Burroughs when he came to London in 1982 for *The Final Academy*. I won't reiterate the whole story of the series of events and who was involved, as I have done that only recently both in print and online (on *Beatdom* website, for instance: http://www.beatdom.com/?p=2022), but what is relevant here is that I invited along as part of the entourage that met Burroughs when he, James Grauerholz, and John Giorno arrived in the U.K. But all was clearly not well with the Beat Godfather: he had gone straight from the airport to the hotel room and then pretty much straight to bed, junk-sick and in a sulk, and word was that he wasn't coming out until his medical needs were seen to. I didn't know quite what the plan had been, or what had gone wrong, but later I understood that rather than risk scoring street junk, there was meant to be a doctor arranging a prescription to cover his requirements for the visit, who obviously hadn't come through in time. Later still I discovered that through the efforts of various well-meaning friends, Burroughs had gone on the Methadone Maintenance Program in New York as an alternative to the hazards of illegal dope, and remained on it until the day he died – but at the time I was amazed to find how much of an open secret it was that he was drug dependent once more.

I can only add that it was a given for anybody that was admitted to the Burroughs circle that even if you didn't directly partake of the junk itself, you were expected to be cool and keep quiet. I don't ever remember meeting anybody who had a problem with that. I guess we all understood that it was part of the price of admission, of the Johnson Code. I was even an accidental witness to the shell game of spin that could surround it: one time I was a low-profile bystander while Mr. Burroughs sat patiently and politely answering questions put to him from a pair of earnest supplicants who wanted to inquire about the efficacy of apomorphine as a treatment for drug addiction. What they didn't realize was that the reason why Mr. Burroughs hadn't been able to make their earlier appointment, and they had been told to come back later, was that he'd been waiting to score, but now that his pharmaceutical requirements had been taken care of he was patient and graceful. Oh the irony.

In closing, I just want to say for the record that my writing this is not intended in any way to denigrate William Burroughs, detract from what I still consider to be his significance as a writer, or even apportion any sort of blame or responsibility, and it is certainly not intended as any kind of judgment or criticism of anybody who was close to him in those years. After all, I can understand only too readily that for anybody to broadcast the fact they are using – or have resumed using – illegal drugs is obviously a bad idea, practically speaking, and that must go double for someone with a notorious reputation and a history of legal difficulties in no small part relating to their pharmaceutical preferences. If I wax nostalgic and lean in a certain direction, I can almost even still half-believe the kind of line that I doubtless glibly accepted without question as an eager young fan, namely that for William *Naked Lunch* Burroughs – arguably the most famous junkie alive at the time – to have kicked junk had to be good for morale, and might even serve as a positive example to others who were struggling. Almost...

The trouble is, whatever he may have thought back in the heady days of his early reading tours the "convenient lie" of his "cure" did not sit well with the man himself. In a diary entry of March 22, 1997 (less than six months before he passed from this life), after a recurring dream of the cheap rooming house world of the old time junkies he had first met in the pages of Jack Black's *You Can't Win* and would later come to know so well himself, in a moment of unflinching self-lacerating honesty he writes:

> *"How can anyone endure this furtive, precarious life without junk? Shows me the full power that junk has over me, lying hypocrite that I am. 'Oh yes, oh yes – I'm off the junk.' Knowing that abrupt withdrawal from Methadone, 60 milligrams per day, would in all likelihood be fatal."*

Although these words would not be published until after his death, in the collection of his final journals, *Last Words*, Burroughs eventually did what he always had to do: tell the truth, even if it reflected badly on him.

Night Shift, Richmond Station
Theater Monologue from 1986

by Zeena Schreck

We knew what we were doing. We did this all the time. See, Carl rented a little one-bedroom up north where he could get away from the family to write. It was all worked out. Sometimes we did different things. But for the most part it was pretty much the same. No use tryin' to tell you why; you wouldn't understand. Or, maybe you would.

That night it was cold and raining hard. I gave him his choice of rope - that one there - and wrapped it around his neck. That end, with the hook on it, had to attach in the ring he fastened in the ceiling. We got a good fire going, so I wouldn't get cold. The smell of the wood burning was thick.

I turned away, to put the record on. That's what he liked; for me to turn away from him and act like he wasn't there. And the music had to be just right. Like I was alone going about my business, dancing or... whatever... but to never look at him while he stood in the corner on... the stool.

So I'd just dance around all sexy in front of the long mirror or, y'know, change lingerie and stockings n' stuff, while I had a little glass of champagne or something. Maybe pretend that I was talking on the phone to my friends about what a little pussy he was, who never knew what I was up to in my silk stockings and midnight-blue nightie, while he stayed tied

36

up all night!

I always knew when he'd get hot. That's when I'd hear the thump of the stool hit the floor. I was supposed to get to him quick, get the stool back up so we could unfasten the hook in time. We had it all worked out. I'd get him steady while we got him out of the noose and over to the bed to check him over.

Then he'd want me to leave the room until he... finished... y'know? So, then he'd come into the other room where I was when he was ready to serve me. That would arouse him again. And after he'd already had one... well, he could, shall we say, have more stamina.

But this time... that night, when I heard the stool hit the floor, everything slowed to an IV drip. I turned and he was swinging, kicking, kicking - I don't know why! I don't know WHY he did that!

I screamed, "Carl - what the fuck are you doing?!"

I bent over to pick up the stool but the stool was under his feet. His feet were thrashing. I couldn't reach. Couldn't get it fast enough. He jerked and his foot knocked me in the face! Everything went black.

Knocked me out cold for what felt like centuries. But, Oh, God, when I came to, he wasn't swinging anymore. He was just so still. Everything was so still. The record was stuck at the end.

Think all that ER nursing prepares you? This is not on the list. I didn't know what to do - just went into autopilot. I know how to move bodies in disasters. Got a knife, cut the rope. Yeah, I took him to Lands End - where our first date was. Neither of us were supposed to be there. Nobody knew we were there. Just like at the cabin. You know, he used another name when he was at the cabin. What would you have done? I waited 'til about 4 to do it, for the rain to stop.

It was quiet then.

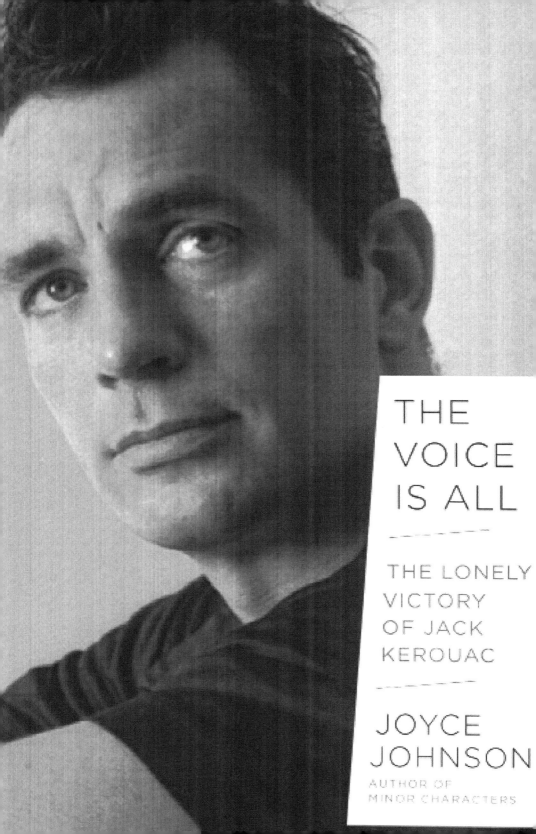

THE
VOICE
IS ALL

THE LONELY
VICTORY
OF JACK
KEROUAC

JOYCE
JOHNSON

AUTHOR OF
MINOR CHARACTERS

The Voice Is All
Joyce Johnson Talks About Her Latest Book

Interview by David S. Wills

Joyce Johnson's role in Beat history is too often viewed simply as that of Jack Kerouac's girlfriend. There is surprise when one first learns that she was a novelist in her own right, and disdain for her position as a scholar of the Beat Generation. She is derided as "milking" her brief relationship with Kerouac. The irony is that her book, *Minor Characters*, brought to light some of the experiences of the women of the Beat Generation, and the extent to which they have been marginalized.

But Johnson's contribution to Beat studies have been tremendously important, and *Minor Characters* has become a classic. In her subsequent works, *Doors Wide Open* and *Missing Men*, Johnson continued to add to our understanding of the Beats and their literature through a decidedly personal approach, offering a rare insider's guide to the Beat Generation and the life of Kerouac, whom she dated between 1957-58.

Thus there was the expectation that in her most recent book, *The Voice is All: The Lonely Victory of Jack Kerouac*, we would once again be treated to a subjective and personal account of the author, most likely focusing on the two years during which time they were romantically involved. But that was not the case. Johnson has taken advantage of the recent opening of the Jack Kerouac Archive at the New York Public Library's Berg Collection in order to research a period of his life that ended six years prior to their meeting. She has chosen to study only a short period in his life, and to examine it from an entirely different angle than that attempted by any of the countless previous biographers and critics.

Why focus on the period up until 1951?

I intended from the start to make the development of Jack's writing - from his acquisition of English, which was a second language for him, through the discoveries that led him to his becoming exactly the writer he wanted to be - the central focus of my book. By the time I began writing about 1951, I felt that by following Jack through the series of breakthroughs after *On the Road* that resulted five months later in the writing of *Visions of Cody*, the book he considered his masterpiece, I had told not only a complete story, but the most important story about Jack, in a way that cast light upon the future years I did not cover.

What inspired you to examine the importance of his cultural and linguistic background, and to what extent did that inform his style of writing?

Curiously, although it is a well known fact that Jack was Franco-American, the implications of his cultural heritage were not explored in previous biographies. I first became aware of how important it might be in early 1980's when I read *Kerouac: A Chicken Essay* by the French-Canadian poet, Victor Lévy-Beaulieu. That book captured something about Jack that I had felt intuitively when I knew him. When I decided to write the biography, this was another theme I wanted to explore, and I found a lot that related to it in Jack's papers, since it was a constant preoccupation of his. There's an extraordinary entry in a 1945 journal, for example, where he writes that although he can understand and appreciate "American richness," it will never be his because he is only "half-American." During the years when he was growing up, Franco-Americans were a despised minority (in New England they were called "white niggers"); in *On the Road* and in his journals, Jack refers to his "white ambitions" - language only someone who did not feel "white" would use.

Jack's family spoke the French-Canadian dialect known as *joual,* and he did not learn his first words of English until he was six. Although he succeeded in mastering English, and in the process forgot some of his French, the *joual* seems to have been his interior language, and writing evidently involved a kind of process of translation. That process gave him an exceptional sensitivity to sound. After years of keeping the French out of his American voice, in 1951 he began to let it back in - first in *On the Road*, which was preceded in March of 1951 by a novella written in French, where I believe Jack found the voice he would use only a few weeks later for the narrator of the novel he had been unsuccessfully struggling to write for the past four years...It's those French overtones that give Sal Paradise's voice its special sound.

You've said you were less than satisfied with previous biographies of Jack. How does yours 'set the record straight'?

It is only in the last few years that scholars have had access to the Kerouac Archive, which contains such a remarkable record of Jack's life and creative development in journals, letters and manuscript. This is essential material for biography. Without it, past biographers had to rely largely on oral history, which was valuable but not necessarily reliable, and on what Jack wrote about his life in his novels, which could often be misleading, since his books are indeed works of fiction. Based largely on anecdotal material gathered from interviews, the books presented a picture of Kerouac in which the emphasis seemed to be upon his dysfunctionality and the extraordinarily dedicated artist that he actually was often got buried in a mass of sensational details.

The book is touted as a bit of an "insider's guide" due to your relationship with Kerouac, but you first met him six years after the period your book examines. How did you go about researching the book?

My book is the product of fifty years of reflection on Jack, during which my understanding grew with everything new that I learned. Although the relationship I had with Jack when I was in my early twenties lasted less than a couple of years, it happens to be one of his longest relationships with a woman. During that period I saw him at his best and at his worst, and got to know the quiet, tender, extremely vulnerable person Jack was when he was sober; when I showed him portions of my first novel, I experienced personally his unfailing generosity to other writers. At seventy-seven, I am hardly sentimental about Jack, but I still feel deep sad affection for him, and my intimate knowledge of him definitely shaped my point of view when it came to writing *The Voice Is All*. But every biography is inescapably shaped by the writer's point of view, which is why each biography of the same person will tell a different story.

I began working on *The Voice Is All* early in 2008 and for the next three years spent two days a week taking notes at the Berg Collection at the New York Public Library, where I kept running into other Kerouac scholars...I went through Jack's papers chronologically while my writing kept pace with my research, and became rather fanatical about establishing an exact chronology for the events in his life, which I felt was very badly needed...I read up on Franco-American life in the United States, and also read some of the writers who were most important to Jack - especially Saroyan, Thomas Wolfe, and Louis Ferdinand Céline.

Was it tough with the restrictions imposed by the Sampas family?

The restrictions upon how much I could quote seemed a challenge at first, but I have ended up feeling the book is all the better for them. I had to choose each quote very carefully and concentrate upon its meaning, which I think has given my book a certain clarity. The narrative, unbroken by long quotes, also has a unity of tone that I think is all to the good. I was very pleased when one reviewer compared my book to "a big Russian novel," because that's how it felt to me while I was living inside it and writing it.

The Beatest Photo

This photo was taken by Jerry Aronson, director of the magnificent documentary, The Life and Times of Allen Ginsberg, which will be re-released on DVD in 2013, and received a glowing review in Beatdom #9. He generously agreed to allow Beatdom the rights to reprint it. It appears in the Photo Gallery, one of the DVD's many special features.

It is surely among the most inclusive of all photos in Beat History. Taken in July 1982 on the porch of Allen Ginsberg's Boulder home, during the Naropa Institute's Kerouac Conference, it features some of the biggest names in mid-20th century American literature. From top left we have Peter Orlovsky, Lawrence Ferlinghetti, William S. Burroughs, Gregory Corso, John Clellon Holmes, Allen Ginsberg, Carl Solomon, and Robert Frank. These men wrote, published, and inspired some of the most groundbreaking and culturally significant work in modern literary history.

For more information on Jerry Aronson and The Life and Times of Allen Ginsberg, visit www.allenginsbergmovie.com.

Batman
by Velourdebeast

After my boyfriend left me
I developed a strong desire to cover the back of my neck with scarves or
hoodies.
There was a stinging at my brain stem.
I was eating lunch with my coworkers months later when one of the men,
a fellow engineer,
wouldn't stop talking about a shooting at a Batman movie in Colorado.
"This dude just dropped the baby and took off,
and a complete stranger jumped on the girlfriend and her other kid,
and then he got shot,
meanwhile another guy covered a woman,
and then that guy got shot,
and his friend covered him,
and then that guy got shot."
Each came to the conclusion that he would jump on top of a woman or
child
to shield them from bullets.
I said nothing,
and I felt my shoulders drawing up.
I wanted to pull them over me like a blanket and fall asleep.

Fare Thee Well
by Michael Hendrick

You used to be the funny guy;
now you are the joke.
We used to hang together
'til you noosed up all the rope.
Your words all splutter sideways
in coughs of blood-laced smoke.
Then you ask why
I don't come by
in girlie little notes.

Dive bar drunkie,
the shit sticks to your shoe.

Live your stain of whiskey.
Watch your socks fill up with piss.
You could have had the picket fence
and family that you miss.
Look into the mirror,
see your father looking back -
then try to drown the fucker out
with your emphysemic hack.

Dive bar drunkie,
there's nothing left to do.

Herbert Huncke:
Times Square Superstar

by Spencer Kansa

I first met Herbert Huncke in the spring of 1992, during a layover in New York, en route to visiting William S. Burroughs down at his home in Lawrence, Kansas. Shortly after my arrival in Manhattan, I received a phone call at my hotel from Burroughs' *consigliere*, James Grauerholz, who graciously welcomed me to America. During our conversation, I joked how I'd been hanging around Times Square, looking for Huncke, deep down figuring that the guy was long gone by now. However James informed me that, on the contrary, Huncke was very much alive, and could be found playing poker most evenings at the Chelsea Hotel.

Excited by the chance to meet this legendary catalyst of the Beats, I headed out from my Midtown hotel that evening, nightwalking the charged, narcotic streets of New York – you got high just from being on them. I was amazed by how deserted the place became at night, and the fact that you can walk entire blocks of the teeming metropolis - inhabited by over a million people - and not see a soul. The sidewalks fresh from a recent rain shower, glistening under the orange haze of street lights. The skyscrapers as broad and impressive as Robert Mitchum's shoulders. The scenery so familiar, it begins to feel like you're wandering through a vast, disused movie set.

I eventually arrived at the Chelsea around ten that evening. With its faded grandeur and ruined beauty, the hotel was now a dirty old dame of a building. I asked after Huncke at the front desk and was told me that he hadn't dropped by that night but I was free to wait for him in the front lobby on the chance that he would.

Sat on a couch in the lobby, I got talking to Nina, a spaced-out, Mogadon-voiced broad, who, I later learnt, was one of the main drug connections in the place. Studying her puffy, heavily made-up face, I zeroed in on her staring eyes, which never blinked as she ran through the gamut of famous names she had met here. Once Nina left, I passed the time surveying the art trophies on the wall - I dug Larry Rivers best. Then I witnessed former Warhol actress Viva Superstar swanning out of the building, trailing domestic melodrama, while moustachioed ex-Warhol dancer Victor Hugo pirouetted in through the lobby with gay abandon.

I'd subsequently ask Huncke about Warhol, imagining he would've been an ideal candidate for the pop artists' rogues gallery of outsiders and misfits, and was surprised when he admitted that he and Warhol hadn't gotten along at all.

Over an hour passed and there was still no sign of Huncke but eventually a gambling gal pal of his, Linda Twigg, did show up and put me on the phone with him. My ears were soon greeted by a woebegone, Droopy Dog voice that was both mournful and yet had a strangely suggestive quality to it. After a pleasant back-and-to we agreed to meet the next day.

At that time, Huncke was living in a basement on a row of bombed-out brownstones on East Seventh Street, in the derelict wastelands of Alphabet City. His bunker was just down a block from Ginsberg's legendary apartment, where the famous photos of Kerouac and Burroughs skylarking about were taken.

I tapped on the dusty window, as per instructions, and heard the man, himself, shuffling his way down the hallway. He was small with an almost bird-like gait. His gaunt, hollow cheeks, drawn mouth, and sallowed skin billboarding a half-century heroin habit. But it was true what they say; the smack really did seem to have suspended his aging process. It wasn't only his nice head of chestnut brown hair - slicked back fifties style - that made you forget that this was a man in his late seventies. It was also his attire – blue jeans and a dark blue bomber jacket. In fact, it struck me that

47

he could've been Iggy Pop's long lost father, something I would tease him about later (Actually, Huncke held out hopes of one day meeting the still stage-diving Stooge, but I don't think anything ever came of it.).

It was only my second day in New York, and I was already breaking bread with Herbert Huncke - the Times Square superstar. A man who's gritty autobiography read like a real life *film noir*. The vice-ridden Virgil who guided Burroughs, Kerouac, and Ginsberg through the nocturnal New York underworld of the 1940s, a demimonde of dark delights. The seasoned *schmecker* who administered Burroughs his first shot of morphine, who's plaintive expression of feeling *beat* - tired, exhausted, and worn-out - was reinterpreted by Kerouac, and transformed into the uplifting *beatific* spirit for their post-war generation.

The next seven hours spent in his company sped by in a cocaine-fueled gabfest, as I lapped up the hard-won lore laid down by this wily, old street fox. Huncke certainly lived up to his legend. I was treated to a personal reading and listened, enraptured, to his first-hand accounts of watching my heroine, Billie Holiday, crooning her heart out at Birdland; Or the yarns spun about his old partner in crime Phil White - aka 'The Sailor 'in Burroughs' *Naked Lunch* - and the trips they took abroad, including a memorable stopover in London just after the war.

Prompted by my name, Huncke recounted how he once had a black boyfriend called Spencer, who had worked for Gore Vidal and, on the

subject of monikers, he reminisced how black <u>pimps</u> used to crack up when he told them *his* surname, because it sounded so similar to "honky."

Unsurprisingly, given his *modus operandi*, law and order was a recurring subject for Huncke and, during our first encounter, he rapped about the Tompkins Square Park riots that broke out four years earlier when the heavy-handed cops waded in to destroy the makeshift "tent city" that the homeless had established there. With vexation he described the sickening scenes of violence as cops cracked heads with their billy clubs and made sure their badges were covered up so they couldn't be identified and later prosecuted.

In the middle of our powwow Huncke's friend, Dimitri, showed up. He was also a musician, like myself, and came across as a soulful dude, with gypsy features and Andre Agassi eyes. Over more snorts, the newcomer brought up the, then-hot topic of the new Joe Camel advertisement campaign, and they discussed how the chain smoking camel's cartoon face appeared redolent of both male *and* female genitalia, depending on how you looked at it. At one point Huncke even fished a handgun out of a trunk – a .45 - and showed it off. And I was happy to be used as a go-between, when he asked if I would pass on his new address to Burroughs when I met up with him.

Although suspicious of Burroughs' sometimes caustic pronouncments - "that's just Bill being Bill", Huncke sniffed - whenever he spoke about his old confrère it was always in glowing terms. Like many, he considered Burroughs one of the world's greatest writers and you got the impression that Herbert felt both grateful and bemused to have been taken up, originally, as a streetwise fount of knowledge by these budding literary lions.

In contrast to Burroughs' mordant misanthropy, a bare-bones humanity poured out of Huncke's own writing, and my favourite memories of him were when he'd read from one of his books, be it *Huncke's Journals*, *Guilty of Everything* or *The Evening Sun Turned Crimson*. It was riveting listening to him recite his poignant and compassionate portraits of the often-marginalized characters he had known in his life, such as the heartrending story of Elsie John, a six and a half foot tall hermaphrodite sideshow freak, who took the tenderfoot Huncke under her wing, and introduced him to the joys of junk. Huncke's relationship with Elsie ended with her arrest and, on a chilling cliffhanger, the reader is left to imagine the fate worse than death that awaits the vulnerable androgyne, as she's about to be thrown to the wolves in the prison bullpen.

Huncke wrote how, after taking a shot of heroin, he would close his eyes and his mind became absorbed with visions of people and places, past times and old faces. A vanishing world of vaudeville hotels leftover from the Wild West. A sleazy backstreet bar in New Orleans, where a trick once paid him to watch as he balled a negro whore. A compendium of clandestine folktales drawn from the underbelly of a lost America that was magically brought back to life in the pages of Huncke's memoirs; or passed on, via the oral tradition, at his public and private readings.

I especially loved his descriptions of the opium dens he frequented in Chinatown back in the old days. It was via Huncke that I learnt that the term "hip" derived from opium eaters would lay *on their hip*, sideways on, as they sucked down the soporific smoke from their smouldering pipes.

In common with most opiate users Huncke could be a real sweetheart when he was smack-sated, but the more he started jonesin' for his next fix, the crankier he'd become. And, if left unassuaged, he could turn into a crabby curmudgeon. But it all came with the territory. Huncke possessed an incredible metabolism. He remains the only guy I've ever met in my life who would do cocaine to get some sleep!

Like Burroughs, he railed against the evil and idiocy of drug prohibition and the phoney war on drugs; together with the demonization of them by a histrionic media. He had earned his insights.

Born in 1915, in Greenfield, Massachusetts, but raised in the middle class environs of Chicago, Huncke was barely in his teens when he fled his broken home and all the restrictions it placed upon him. He set out, like a depression era Huck Finn, armed only with a cigar box containing a toothbrush, a razor, a handkerchief, and a clean pair of socks. Seeking "peace of mind" and possessed with a wanderlust to explore "'the big, bad, beautiful world," he hit the road, hitchhiking with his thumb or riding the rails with hobos and bums across all forty-eight American states.

Under the tutelage of Runyonesque reprobates, he began engaging in prostitution and low level larceny - nefarious misadventures that provided him with two pivotal experiences in life - his first joint and his first blow job. Although he could enjoy such hedonistic pleasures while he was still honing his street wits, the outlaw life is a precarious business, and one disastrous night's stay in Los Angeles culminated in an arrest that left him with a lifelong loathing for The City of Angels.

New York City, on the other hand, was a different matter, and it was there, in 1939, that Huncke's wayfaring came to end. Nestled in the bohemian bosom of the Big Apple, he felt a true sense of belonging at last and, for the first time in his life, he could walk around Forty-Second Street and hold his head up high.

Living the hard-knock life of a junkie and petty criminal extorted a terrible price though, and the consequences of his risky choices meant he had to endure the long-drawn-out misery of serving time in such brutal hell holes as Sing Sing. It was while incarcerated that he learned that the difference between a faggot and a hustler in jail is "a faggot is everyone's property."

In the autumn of 1994, Huncke flew into London to undertake a short reading tour in promotion of his books and a new spoken word CD, *From Dream to Dream*. We hung out while he was in town and I visited him

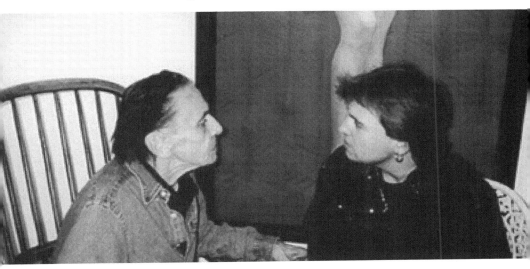

again in New York that Christmas.

By then he was ensconced at the Chelsea Hotel, having moved there that summer following the tragic death of his buddy, Louis Cartwright - a gifted but downward spiraling poet, who was stabbed to death during a street fight in the East Village, reportedly over panhandled money.

Huncke was living in Room 828 - a tiny shoebox with a single cot, a sink, and a window view of neighboring rooftops and apartments, his rent paid at the charitable behest of those psychedelic sons of beatniks, The Grateful Dead. I was taken aback when Huncke confided that the hotel management didn't like him. I couldn't understand why as he was, by then, the only interesting person left in this obscenely overpriced roach pit. When I inquired, he muttered, with resignation, "I'm not good for business."

The final time I visited Huncke at the Chelsea, he'd just returned from the Kerouac Festival in Lowell, where he had read alongside Patti Smith. A framed poster, picturing the two of them, hung proudly on his wall. Huncke was also basking in the latter-day glory being bestowed upon him by the Whitney Museum, who treated him as a VIP guest at their *Beat Culture and The New America* retrospective.

It was great to see Huncke getting some legitimate recognition at last. *Herbert and Louis,* a deeply affecting documentary, directed by Laki Vazakas, was already in the pipeline, and Huncke had recently been interviewed by the BBC for a TV documentary on the pioneering sexologist Doctor Alfred Kinsey, who, back in the mid-forties, had paid Huncke to solicit the colorful denizens of Times Square - including Burroughs and Ginsberg - to be interviewed for his groundbreaking report into *Sexual Behavior in the Human Male.*

Typically, the book publishers waited until after Huncke's death to release his collected works. A crying shame, as Huncke could have sorely used that moolah while alive, but, alas, the old adage about how the best work is worth most after the workman can't be paid followed him to the crematorium.

One of my lasting memories of Huncke dates from that period. It occurred the night before I flew home to London, and he begged me for a favor. Herbert had an appointment at the methadone clinic the next day and asked if I could supply a sample of my urine for him to take there, as his was bastardized with traces of smack, coke, and God knows what else. I was clean at the time and more than happy to lend a, ahem, hand. In fact, it was a dubious honor.

Huncke always used the sink in his room to take a splash, but I passed on that and went to the john at the end of the landing. After I presented him with the beaker of pure piss, Huncke gave me a peck on the lips and promised to call me in the morning before I left for my flight. It was then, as I was descending the staircase, that the screwy thought hit me: God! I hope that *is* what he's using it for! I sure hope he's not guzzling it!

Baby American Dream

by Charles Lowe

The tree prefers calming, but the wind keeps blowing. I often say this to my husband. What does it matter, he is in real estate. Not that I'm complaining. I am in the Vincent Van Gogh Estates, so named for the softly colored brick walls located next to a newly built subway stop, which can be seen from a fancy veranda, overlooking a solitary palm trees in need of regular watering but is still dying. Who would be crazy enough to plant a palm tree in a northern city, which leads me to my story? It is called Baby American Dream, my story.

Well, it is not my story exactly. It's my mom's, well, what do you expect? In any case, I am sitting on my veranda, watching the different passersby hustle into an underground tunnel (I've never taken a subway; we have a driver) when ma calls me. She says, "Gui-niu (that's her name for me), do you want a Baby American Dream?"

Well, I do think it's strange, but do I say anything? Well, you know me, when have I ever? Well, she says to me, I know the daughter of a friend. She (the daughter) has got a website. I say, that's good. Ma gives me an address. It comes up with what else - Baby American Dream. I say, ma, I got it. She says, that's my Gui-niu.

My backbone and spine hurt. But I'm thinking, what else. I am her girl. So I say now what? "Well, do you think elephant tusks don't grow

53

from a dog's mouth?"

I have no idea what ma means and smile. Ridiculous, huh, I am talking over the phone, so I smile at a subway visitor. He's a foreigner with a shaft of red hair that peels over his left eye. He doesn't see me, so I feel comfortable and fully let loose my smile. I've been told my smile is beautiful. It is a bright jewel. It is like a wave in the Pacific, bending into the wide open sands. Anyways, I wait. Finally, after mom's given me enough wisdom to chew on, she says to invite the salesperson over for a talk with my husband. I don't say a word and look through Baby American Dream further:

> For only 50000 USD, a Chinese mom along with her mom
> can transit to the United States and its territories so as to
> meet a real doctor and birth a REAL US CITIZEN.

That's what's scrolled on the website in large red and blue thick letters. Interesting, I think and start to consider how the thick and somewhat curvy message can be possible. I'm not even carrying. But I know ma. She's not me, a girl with an empty tortoise shell for a skull. She's got the scheme and is already two moves ahead; mom's a natural go player. I've seen her roll up lines of plastic black circles, a big smile flitting across her face. That woman is unafraid to smile.

So I tell my husband to set aside Sunday late afternoon. It's our only time alone. Husband usually spends Sunday mornings at the office, and mom comes by around six but arrives early then around one or so with a plastic bag and insists I steam the fish. Mom starts with the Goubuli buns, big fat saucers stuffed with pork and bok choy that mom won't let me have a hand in until I'm a woman (by that, she means pregnant). Mom smiles: granted, not the smile that may be offered freely to a subway visitor who won't see you for at least another generation.

No, the kind that husband uses to close a real estate deal after he discovers the client's got buyer's remorse. My husband has closed several in the spacious living room of our two-floor villa, and believe me, it's not an infrequent occurrence especially when the client's put down for a second home and has to dip into the savings meant for a medical emergency - hospitals won't take anyone without cash in hand, not emergency rooms, not if your body is covered with burn marks, you feel the burn marks inside your eyelids and you are blind. I often have that nightmare whenever my husband talks about his phantom homes. Phantom homes haven't been built yet. When they're built, my husband explains in his most thorough voice, they can be turned over quickly, for a lot more than if they were dreams. But for now, the two of us have to wait and hope that our fancy villa with the perfect view of busy subway visitors doesn't evaporate like it was a dream.

Every time, I see a construction crane, I have that vision. I see the crane swinging like the jaws of some animal (not exactly a dog, I am still thinking of mom's riddle). Anyways, I put away that nightmare and get ready for Baby American Dream. Yes, we are still talking about my mom's plan to get me with a child, a real American, and though I do want my time alone with my husband and maybe he does too, he says - well he doesn't say, but I feel he doesn't love real estate. His lips have thinned, and his skin has lost clear feeling. When mom brought us together (actually she and a workmate, but mom calls husband her gift to me, no joke!), he looked like he had been dusted with shiny grains of sand.

Mom is happy though, let me tell you. She comes to our apartment extra early, so I had no time that day to survey the subway visitors disappearing into their separate caves. I have to set up our kitchen. And let me tell you, I'm not a typical Chinese girl. I may be on the surface, following husband and mom, blah, blah, but underneath I'm not that soft girl who stares at you from a warmly tiled veranda. I hate cooking. I hate cooking really very much. When mom is off at auntie's dive in the downtown, auntie is our poor relation but those two are like two crows babbling when they get together: I like to order out - don't be shocked - pre-prepared dumplings right from a stand. I don't leave the apartment compound, not even the apartment.

You see, our apartment has a feature, a telephone pad with a TV screen to the right, and I look into the guard's eyes and freely say, "Can you send for a dozen tofu dumplings?" I giggle (like a school girl, you won't believe it), "I'm watching my figure."

The guard's mouth goes open. There is no elephant tusk growing from his lips. Twenty minutes later, a kid shows up with a plastic bag. I see his palm. It is soft and unwrinkled like the shore of a Pacific island that nobody will ever visit, so I slip an extra ten. He sees it and pushes it back into my palm. I have on my husband's smile. The kid doesn't notice. I hear his bike tires scraping against the back metal door of the apartment; they don't clean that, and it doesn't look as though a sophisticate like Van Gogh could walk through it; then, the kid's gone, and I can swallow each fried dumpling, let the grease stick to my tongue; then smile freely at the subway visitors until they disappear into a tunnel draped with starlight. But not this Sunday, mom is steaming Goubuli buns, the steam providing the nearly transparent kitchen tile with a very thin tissue. I don't like seeing my kitchen disordered and want to tell mom of my other habit - my secret habit (I don't tell mom or husband about my need to purchase street dumplings. It's silly I know, but I don't just the same).

We wait. At 4:30pm, husband comes home: his Arnold Palmers swung over his meaty shoulders. Mom says she approves of golf. All Westerners play that game. It's a good way to make guanxi, and husband agrees, he says connections are the key to hustling off luxury villas in Vincent Van Gogh or other luxury lodgings.

Finally, the woman comes over and shows us a brochure coated in plastic and promising that for 70000 bucks (the price's been raised) we can have an all-expense paid trip to Saipan. Then, she shows various sites from the island of Saipan, a dizzying flyspeck in the middle of the Pacific. The island has rich clay cliffs, she tells us excitedly, off which the Japanese soldiers jumped rather than face the invading American Marines, and I decide right then and there, listening to her gentle voice while surveying a wind calming down a very thin palm tree on a very still beach, that ma has another good one, so guess what, I say before husband can get in the first or second word, that I think we should do it. Mom smiles, not like she was closing a phantom deal, but freely like she was eying a subway visitor down a tunnel. Did I tell you that you cannot see inside the lit tunnel from the warmly tiled veranda of our two-floor villa?

Husband doesn't appear too bothered. He's used to women pushing him around; he told me once when we were still dating that I was lucky for that reason. I believed him and still do. So, he signs the contract which requires a down payment of 1000 bucks. The woman carries around a bank card machine, which she takes out from a plastic shopping bag and bends down. I watch my husband studying the nearly invisible lines creasing her short white pants suit. The skin on her calves looks unshaved, and I wonder if she's married, if she's had many lovers. Did I tell you, she's in her twenties, and these little empresses, that's what we call them, have no shame. Mom says she knows a twenty something girl who's already had three lovers, and I ask mystified, isn't the girl worried about a husband?

"These young men, what do they know, they figure if the girl has spread her legs enough, you know, she'll be more skilled at" mom guffaws, "dumpling making," which makes me wonder if mom knows my secret.

So we're locked in, husband has agreed within two years to transport me to a small U.S. territory, no more than a speck, where I can birth a little dream, though the girl warns us (she has eyelids that vanish beneath her thinly grained skin) that the kid will never have the chance to be an Obama. "FOR THAT," the girl clicks her tongue professionally (how do you do that?), "YOU HAVE TO BIRTH YOUR LITTLE DREAM IN THE FORMAL PART OF THE STATES WHICH FOR AN EXTRA 50,000 USD..."

Mom shuts the girl off right there. No Obama. Mom's maybe five moves ahead, but the girl pretends not to be listening. She's studying mom's finely dusted Goubuli (did I tell that you can barely see its floury skin?) and opens the brochure to Obama, Malia, Sasha, and Michelle; Sasha at Obama's knees, Michelle affectionately touching her husband's firm and strong palm. And I start to consider maybe I'm robbing my Baby American Dream. Who knows, maybe I am, but the girl sees me and knows that elephant tusks cannot grow out a dog's mouth - hey, that does sound nice - so shuts off the screen and snaps her Apple shut.

The rest is simple. Husband adds his name to the contract. Mom treats him like a hero. Mom has a rather large chest, I do not, and she puts on an extra bit of lipstick and, I'm not ashamed to say, flirts with my husband. Her eyes fixed into his eyes as he tells the four of us (the girl stays for supper) how he convinced another couple to buy a phantom.

"Isn't it hard," mom says admiringly, "to get a family to put its hospital fund into an apartment that is a bit of... in fact... thin air?"

She says all this drawing out each word like a bubble beneath a cliff that a bunch of Japanese soldiers jumped off when the other choice was to meet an American. I start to picture the clay cliffs, then the endless and very thin lines of sand. Then, I visit my future. I'm carrying Baby American Dream. Only it's like I am that girl in the brochure, carrying a baby though my hips remain nicely sculpted and my stomach flat, and I am wearing fashionable shades like Obama jaunting off a well-protected jet, Michelle also with shades on and by his side, her skin against his finely grained skin, and I feel what it must feel like when your life holds endless possibilities. So I start smiling freely like I know what it's like to have elephant tusks grow from the mouth and forget to add a word.

Down These Mean Streets: Raymond Chandler's L.A.

by Chris Dickerson

Certain cities belong to a few writers. They may not own the towns exclusively, but they've put their stamp on them so indelibly in their books and stories that anybody who writes about the places after them can't help but live in their shadow. Dashiell Hammett long ago claimed San Francisco. Those chilly, fog-wreathed sidewalks where Sam Spade pursues the elusive Maltese Falcon reek of Prohibition Era corruption and Barbary Coast intrigue. You can still hear the echo of the pistol shot in the back alley where Spade's partner, Miles Archer, was gunned down.

New York belongs to Pete Hamill. Not only in his three Sam Briscoe private eye novels, but in anything Hamill writes; be it journalism or fiction, the soggy heat of a summer's day lingers over Times Square and Forty-second Street, clogs the subways, and mingles with the fumes of trucks and taxis while the Christmas snows turn the metropolis into a hushed, glimmering wonderland.

Robert B. Parker staked out Boston for private detective Spenser, just as surely as London – where it's always 1895 – belongs to the bustling Victorian jungle of Sherlock Holmes, and the narrow, winding streets of Paris, with its cozy cafes and the sluggish Seine, are home to Georges Simenon's Inspector Maigret.

Many writers have tackled the sprawling crazy-quilt that is Los Angeles; John Fante springs to mind, Michael Connelly, and certainly Charles Bukowski, but nobody captured the town better, in seven novels and numerous short stories written between 1933 and 1958, than Raymond Chandler. L.A., pure and simple, is "Chandlertown." When Chandler writes about Los Angeles, you can smell the orange trees, the jasmine, and the eucalyptus on the night wind, feel the breeze sliding across the mountainous landscape from the nearby Pacific Ocean, and see the moon shining down like a hallowed street lamp above the ghostly black palm trees.

What's most remarkable is, in the decades since Chandler was sending his private investigator Philip Marlowe, out on his adventures from an office on Hollywood Boulevard, the place hasn't changed all that much – not the architecture, the people, or the sins committed in the City of Angels.

Chandler was born in 1888 in Chicago, but after his parents split up when he was a boy of seven, his mother, who was Anglo-Irish, took him back to her home in England. He was educated there, returning to America in 1907. Then Chandler drifted. He worked a variety of menial jobs, signed on with a Canadian unit in World War I (when his outfit was shelled by the Germans, he was the only survivor), eventually winding up as the bookkeeper for an oil company in Southern California.

The Depression put an end to that. Chandler's habitual boozing and chasing secretaries might have had something to do with it too, but either way in 1932 he was out of a job, past forty, with a wife eighteen years his senior, and a bleak future.

He decided to become a writer. He'd played around with writing as a young man, scribbling poetry and minor literary reviews. Now – with few other prospects – he went at it with the thoroughness and attention to detail of a dogged (and probably desperate) detective. He read pulp magazines. There were a few hundred of them on the newsstands every week, offering up adventure tales, sci-fi, westerns, horror, sex, and detective stories; plenty of detective stories.

Chandler soon saw that the best of the "hard-boiled" writers was Dashiell Hammett, but Hammett didn't invent the American private eye any more than Chandler did. That distinction probably belongs to a genial hack named Carroll John Daly, whose private detective, Race Williams, burst on the pages of *Black Mask* magazine in 1920 with both .45 pistols blazing, while a breathless flapper cowered behind him. Daly and the rest of his ilk, pounding out stories for the various magazines, showed Chandler the basic formula for keeping a story fast-paced, action-packed. "When in doubt," Chandler noted, "have a man come through the door with a gun in his hand."

Hammett, though, was doing more than just that. Chandler, too, saw the potential for character development, crackling dialogue, social commentary, and a centeredness of time and place in the gaudy, rip-roaring world of the pulps.

Chandler's first sale to *Black Mask* was 1933's "Blackmailers Don't Shoot"; he was paid a whopping $180, a penny a word. His detective isn't called Marlowe, but otherwise, everything else – especially the Los Angeles setting – is in place. Chandler would labor in the pulp salt mines for the next few years, honing his craft, painstakingly writing and rewriting his stories, chipping out a living (he said that at one point, he had nothing to eat for five straight days but soup). By 1939 he was ready for the big jump, and published his first novel: *The Big Sleep*. Its hero is a tall, good looking, well-dressed man, with a sense of integrity, a sharp eye, and a guarded nature, private eye Philip Marlowe. The landscape he moves across is the

city of L.A.

"Down these mean streets a man must go," Chandler wrote in his classic essay, "The Simple Art of Murder." "A man who is not himself mean, who is neither tarnished nor afraid... He is the hero; he is everything... The story is this man's adventure in search of a hidden truth."

Marlowe established his office on Hollywood Boulevard near Ivar Avenue, on the sixth floor of the Cahuenga Building. But Chandler was sometimes cagey with his locations (like when he changed the name of Santa Monica, where a great deal of action takes place in his books, to "Bay City"). The Cahuenga Building is actually a block west from Hollywood and Ivar, on the corner of Hollywood and Cahuenga. Built in 1921, it still stands today, opposite a sign on the corner denoting Raymond Chandler Square, and another sign nearby with a photo of Bogart and Bacall from the film version of *The Big Sleep*, indicating the location as a "Historic Hollywood Site."

Marlowe kept the same office for years, a dusty little two-room suite down at the end of a corridor, with a pebbled glass door on which was stencilled, Philip Marlowe – Investigations. From here, he could look out over the city and gauge its mood:

> *– There was a desert wind blowing that night. It was one of those hot dry Santa Anas that come down through the mountain passes and curl your hair and make your nerves jump and your skin itch. On nights like that every booze party ends in a fight. Meek little wives feel the edge of the carving knife and study their husbands' necks. Anything can happen. –*
>
> (Red Wind, 1938)

But if Marlowe was reluctant to change offices, he changed his place of residence frequently. *The Big Sleep* finds him living in a small apartment with a Murphy bed coming down out of the wall. He lives in the Hobart Arms, "a huge white stucco affair." He lives in an apartment in the "Berglund Arms"; and at one point, he has a place on Vine, a few blocks from his office. By the time of *The Long Goodbye*, he's taken a rented house up a long flight of redwood stairs on Yucca Avenue. Marlowe's frequent moves may reflect Chandler's own. He seemed to be a restless man, and he and his wife moved often, finally settling in La Jolla, many miles down the coast from L.A.

Marlowe stayed in Los Angeles, and Chandler sent him roaming widely. His investigations take him from the quiet suburbs of Pasadena to the opulent estates of Beverly Hills ("the best policed four square miles in California") and Brentwood; from the art deco high-rises of downtown L.A. to the shadowy streets of Bunker Hill; from the gated mansions along Los Feliz Boulevard. out to the ocean and "Bay City."

What's perhaps most interesting is the places Marlowe *doesn't* go. Chandler never sends him into the picturesque and bustling streets of Chinatown, or over into the predominantly Mexican neighborhood of Westlake (now MacArthur) Park, or into the African-American section of Watts, though the opening chapter of *Farewell, My Lovely*, does find Marlowe in an African-American bar downtown, dragged there by the hulking Moose Malloy, in an area that "wasn't all Negro yet." Those locations would seem the ideal geography for an L.A.-based private eye, but Marlowe never goes near them.

It could be because Chandler wasn't a journalist; he wasn't interested in exploring areas he didn't know well. Hollywood and its environs, Chandler knew. But even so, another aspect not explored in detail in the books is the movie industry. Chandler makes some swipes at it in *The Little Sister* – the primary female character is aspiring movie star Mavis Weld – but he never gives "the industry" the beating that, say, Nathaniel West does in *Day Of The Locust*. He certainly could have.

No matter. What Chandler gets, he gets right. Marlowe's Los Angeles is a city of corrupt cops and politicians (like Police Chief "Two Gun" Bill Davis and Mayor Frank Shaw and his brother Joe "The Enforcer" – those aren't Chandler characters, they were real enough in the 1930s), and mobsters like Bugsy Siegel and Meyer Lansky and Mickey Cohen, running the gambling, drugs, and prostitution rackets, and the small-time grifters, the shop girls, and pretty boys who come from all over the country to be famous, to be in the movies, to capture the American Dream.

Little has changed. Davis and Shaw are gone – the city even has a Latino mayor finally – but the cocaine is still in abundance in the Sunset Strip clubs, and the prostitutes stroll nightly on Santa Monica Boulevard. The LAPD may not be as corrupt, but a recent federal bust of the Los Angeles County Sheriff's Department found wide-spread abuse of prisoners and rampant drug-dealing in Men's Central Jail downtown – all of it being done by the sheriffs.

Bugsy Siegel – who said about gangland murders, "We only kill each other" – and Mickey Cohen are history, but now Russian gangs battle it out, and kill each other regularly over in East Hollywood, while the Bloods and Crips have been fighting their turf wars in South L.A. for decades.

And every day the prettiest girls from Pittsburgh, or Portland, or Peoria, get off the bus, or the plane, or the train to become movie stars, or TV stars, while the boys coax their battered over-packed cars up the ramps from the Hollywood Freeway, coming from Denver or Dallas or Duluth, to make it as rock stars, or stand-up comics, or on the next big reality show. They just want to become rich and famous. And the grifters and hustlers and con artists are waiting for them.

> *— When I got home I mixed a stiff one and stood by the open window in the living room and sipped it and listened to the ground swell of traffic on Laurel Canyon Boulevard, and looked at the glare of the big angry city hanging over the shoulder of the hills through which the boulevard had been cut. Far off the banshee wail of police or fire sirens rose and fell, never for very long completely silent. Twenty-four hours a day somebody is running, somebody else is trying to catch him. Out there in the night of a thousand crimes people were dying, being maimed, cut by flying glass, crushed against steering wheels or under heavy car tires. People were being beaten, robbed, strangled, raped and murdered. People were hungry, sick, bored, desperate with loneliness or remorse or fear, angry, cruel, feverish, shaken by sobs. A city no worse than others, a city rich and vigorous and full of pride, a city lost and beaten and full of emptiness. —*

(The Long Goodbye 1953)

Bibliography:
Thorpe, Edward, *Chandlertown: The Los Angeles of Philip Marlowe* (New York: St. Martin's Press, hard cover, 1983)
Silver, Alain, and Ward, Elizabeth, *Raymond Chandler's Los Angeles* (New York: The Overlook Press, 1987)
Gross, Miriam, ed. *The World of Raymond Chandler* (London: Weidenfeld & Nicolson, 1977)

The House of Love
by Kat Hollister

There's a spy in the house of love
cloaked by the specter of lost loves
       he thinks i can't see him

but i've seen the skin stretched
transparent taut over swollen veins
throbbing with the heat of rage

i've glimpsed him in the moonlight
crouched wearily on trembling haunches
sniffing at the air
for the scent of a primal urge

There's a spy in the house of love
he thinks i didn't hear him
on a certain night
lapping at his wounds
       he thinks i didn't see

the sweat glistened footsteps
that circled bedposts
territory marked

he steals lightly his way
watching her from unlit corners
waiting…

waiting for her
to
laugh a little louder
look a little prettier
smile a little easier

Apartheid
by Holly Guran

His eyes were darting
like birds with no place to land
as he crossed the line
leaving work and kitchen
to where the well-clad come
to enjoy a quiet conversation.

His eye caught mine. "Here,"
I offered him a seat, unnerved
because the crash of glass,
his shouting voice and others
from the kitchen had reminded me
of my children fighting.

"Where are you from?"
He named a long street
dividing Boston. I had meant
which island in the Caribbean.
"I'll just sit here," he said.
"Wait for the police."

"Today I baked
so many loaves of bread,
long loaves of bread.
Since morning I been running—
'Go get this, go get that'
they said."

"I'll just sit here.
Wait for the police."

Talking Barefoot
A Chat with Patti Smith

by Michael Hendrick

Patti Smith turns up pretty frequently in *Beatdom*. We hoped she would grace us with an interview and tried doggedly for over a year. We explained to record and book companies that we published material pertaining to Beat literature and that we would like to talk with Patti about her well-known interest in 'Beat' and her association with the Beats *(see Patti Smith and the Beats, Beatdom #7)*. Eventually, we nosed our way to the front of the interview line and, thanks to the release of her latest recording, *Banga*, were able to speak with her. As luck would have it, an email from the recording company publicist came the day before. It said we could not ask about any other subjects besides *Banga*, or maybe her latest book. A download of the new songs came with the message but her work is so rich and dense that it cannot be fully absorbed overnight. It can be enjoyed immediately, though, and is a wonderful album, catchy and deep at the same time.

We were not sure what to ask without sounding like a neophyte, but, as usual, Patti stepped up to save the interview and the day...and that is why she is such a hero to us!

The interview begins as we are told it has been cut by ten minutes:

Columbia Records - She has a very tight schedule, so it will be twenty minutes.

Beatdom - Hello, Patti!

Patti Smith - Hi, good. Good to talk with you. Good Morning.

Beatdom - Happy Mercuralia! We couldn't help but notice that today was Mikhail Bulgakov's birthday.

PS - Yes, it is. It's on our website today.

B - Oh, we hadn't looked yet.

PS - Yes, we saluted him today and you are exactly right. It is his birthday.

B - And why is that important?

PS - Bulgakov is one of the great Russian novelists and playwrights who was suppressed by Stalin and, very simply, he wrote one of the masterpieces of the twentieth century, *The Master and Margarita*. I am not really ready to give a lecture on political culture today but I do like to wish him a Happy Birthday. I think the best way to know Bulgakov is to read him.

B - In terms of your new record, how is this important?

PS - The album title *Banga* came from the dog in *The Master and Margarita*. It was Pontius Pilate's dog and his dog's name was "Banga." The reason I wrote a song for Banga, for those who have not read the book, Pontius Pilate waited on the edge of Heaven for 2000 years to talk to Jesus Christ and his dog, Banga, stayed faithfully by his side and I thought that any dog that would wait 2000 years for his master deserves a song. It's really a song for my band and for the people. It's a high-spirited song, dedicated to love and loyalty. (*It seems worth noting that Mick Jagger wrote the song "Sympathy for the Devil" after reading the same book.-ed.*)

B - Loyalty seems key to your band, everybody who works with you stays with you, it seems.

PS - Unfortunately we lost our pianist Richard Sole. He died of heart failure at the age of thirty-seven. He had a rheumatic heart but I know if Richard was alive, he would be with us and even my bass player Tony Shanahan has been with us since 1995. So I like the camaraderie of the band. They're your team. They're your soldiers. I'm loyal to them and they're loyal to me, as well.

B - We saw Tom Verlaine playing with you on the *Paradise Lost* tour in 1995 and he seemed to have a broken leg. That shows a lot of loyalty.

PS - (*Laughs*) It wasn't quite broken. He had some type of problem but it wasn't broken. I love working with Tom. He is so brilliant and his ability on guitar is expansive. He has his own language and Tom's language and my language are very compatible. Listen to the songs *Nine* and *April Fool* and it's unmistakably Tom.

B - We didn't have much time to listen to the download but, having read that you are working on a song-cycle, we noticed that this album seems very connected in itself.

PS - We had the luxury of working for a longer time period and we had more material so we were able to really put together the material being done that was most compatible with each other...but I am always very schematic. Even when it is very subtle, there are always either one or two themes that run through a record. I always think of records cinematically. They usually begin with something welcoming, sort of an overture and end with an epic, my version of an epic. You're right - this one is very cohesive. It begins with Vespuci; Amerigo entering the New World and finding that the people are much purer and that the land is much purer than they are, even with all of their richer pretensions and then it just moves through different phases and ends with Columbus also entering the New World and seeing such unspoiled beauty and then having a dream of the twenty-first century and the apocalyptic environmental state that we are in.

B - You'll have to forgive us...we were given a message about twenty minutes before the interview that we could only ask about the record and it is so hard to do that, only having heard it a few times.

PS - You don't have to do that...ask what you want. Ask whatever you want because we don't have a lot of time.

B - Thanks! Well, speaking of the album, you wrote the song *Nine* for Johnny Depp and I read interviews where you tell how he helped you by recording the title track, *Banga*. He was close to Allen Ginsberg, so we wondered if you

69

met through Ginsberg?

PS - No…I knew Allen since I was quite young. I met Johnny when he came to one of my concerts a few years ago. We talked and then started off on Allen. We both love books and we spent a lot of time talking about *(Jack)* Kerouac and Dylan Thomas. Johnny has letters of *(Antonin)* Artaud and Dylan Thomas. We spoke a lot about literature and music and became very good friends. A lot of our friendship is book-based.

B - So, about your writing process…oops, we're getting off subject about the album here.

PS - No, No...you don't have to ask about the album!

B - Thanks!...In that case, we'd like to know about your writing process and your detective novel...

PS - I am always writing…always…and always have two or three projects going simultaneously because my mind is so active…like I'm writing poems and always writing little songs and am working on my detective story and some other things. So, I'm always writing. Writing is part of my daily discipline, whether it's for my website (*www.pattismith.net-ed.*) or whatever. I think more than anything else I do...it's the one consistent discipline I've had since I was twelve or thirteen years old that I continue to exercise every day.

I write by hand in my notebooks and on the computer. I don't write so much on the typewriter anymore. I always loved the typewriter, but it's so complicated to get ribbons and things, so I switched over to transcribing on computer - but I initially write in my notebooks.

B - Do you have favorite pens?

PS - I have a very nice pen collection. I have been given beautiful pens by my son and daughter...I have a very nice, small white Montblanc and I have very nice old fountain pens and sometimes it's just a Bic. There is always some pen in my pocket but I sometimes get sentimental towards certain pens. Sometimes I just use a little Uni-Ball. It depends what's in my pocket but I have very nice pens at home. I like those little Montblanc Mozarts. I think they are called the "Mozart Series." They're small, they're ballpoints. They're really good and they have a really nice weight and you can put them in your pocket. That's sort of my upscale pen of choice. I write with whatever is there, though, you know?

Sometimes...if I'm on computer...well, I like to write fast and then go back and edit. I don't like to edit as I am writing and sometimes I can get in a groove at night. When I'm writing late at night sometimes I sit at my computer and, if I'm like writing more of a rap, like if I'm writing something for my website...I usually do my website right on the computer...a lot of times it's just sort of like rappin' and if I'm working on a poem or something like that, I always write by hand.

B - Listening to "Rock N Roll Nigger," the structure seems reminiscent of "Howl." Was that by design?

PS - It's just what we did. I always acknowledge the people that influence me or inspire me but I'm not really conscious of exactly how. I just know that I've learned from them but I don't consciously do a piece of work to mirror another piece - if it does, then it's just because someone else will usually pick up on it, probably subconsciously.

B - We read that Allen had a lot of influence on you coming out of retirement some years ago...

PS - Allen was more influential to me when I was younger as a human being, as an activist. He was just so vocal. He was so successful at marshaling people, at gathering large troops of people to speak out against the government, to strike…so that was his major influence on me.

I often talk about Allen. When you do a hundred interviews, it all depends on how they are edited. I've talked about Allen many times - about how, of course, he was instrumental. He called me up; called my house and inspired me. He said that I should come and let the people help me with my grieving process and let my Loved One go on his journey. I've talked about that on the liner notes of my record…many, many times. I'm always doing something for Allen, reading his poems…paying tribute. There is only so much you can say in one little interview but I am always grateful to Allen.

CR - I just want to let you know you have five minutes left.

B - How about the other Beats?

PS - I was very attached to William [Burroughs]. I knew Gregory, Gregory Corso, very well…and Peter Orlovsky. I met Hubert Huncke.

I was very privileged to know these people and I had different relationships with them all. Gregory was very, very important to me in my learning process in how to deliver poems live…and in my reading list.

But William was the one I was most attached to. I just adored him. I had sort of a crush on him when I was younger and he was very, very good to me. He really liked my singing and encouraged me to sing. He used to come to CBGB to see us and, of course, his work inspired me. *Horses*, the opening of *Horses*, with Johnny's confrontation in the locker room, was very inspired by William's *The Wild Boys*. In *The Wild Boys* there is also a Johnny. My Johnny is a continuation of William's Johnny.

William really taught me a lot about how to conduct myself as a human being, you know? Not to compromise and to do things my way. What William always said was, "The most precious thing you have is your name so don't taint it. Build your name and everything else will come. Keep your name clean." I learned a lot from William.

B - We wonder if you have any suggestions on new books to read, things we may be unaware of.

PS - Well, I mean, I think *2666* is our first twenty-first century masterpiece. I think that one *has* to read that book eventually, by (*Roberto*) Bolaño. Right now I am in a (*Haruki*) Murakami world. I'm reading a lot of Murakami. He's really quite entertaining on many levels. It's interesting to be within his world.

B - You pay tribute to so many great writers on your website and you got to hang around with the Beats. We wondered, if you could time travel, who, in the world of literature, you would like to spend time with.

PS - You know it would be fun to hang out with all of those people but I think it would be interesting to hang out with the Apostles, too. That would be very interesting. I'd like to hang out with John and Matthew and see how their minds worked.

It's an interesting thought. It would be nice to move through time and just hang out with them all.

B - So, why John and Matthew?

PS - John wrote *The Revelations* and that says it all. I don't know who could write like that...who had a vision of the great Apocalypse. I'd say that I'd really like to speak with him...and he was beloved by Jesus so he must have been extremely interesting. He must have had a very beautiful quality.

And Matthew was very stoic and he was a good writer, too. He recorded what I think is one of the greatest quotes in *The Bible*. He had the presence of mind to quote, "and, lo, I am always with you, even until the end of the world." (*Matt 28:20-ed.*)

I think that is one of the greatest lines ever...imagine somebody being with you for that long.

CR - Okay, well, that is all the time Patti has.

B - Well, thanks so much for your time, Patti.

PS - Thank you. Bye-bye.

Ironically, we had been cut short just as Patti was referring to all the time in the world - but somehow it was a fitting end to a short but revealing interview! It also gave us time to rethink the meaning of her declaration at the beginning of the song, *Gloria*, "Jesus died for somebody's sins but not mine."

Keep track of Patti on her website at www.pattismith.net. The new recording, *Banga,* is available at the normal outlets, released by Columbia Records. We thank Patti for the time and graciousness she showed us.

Jack Kerouac's Poetry:
Where is the Gold, if There's Gold?

by Chuck Taylor

This paper is a short inquiry into the quality of Jack Kerouac's poetry. Kerouac is an American writer who has maintained an enduring hold on succeeding generations of readers through his long prose works, such as *On the Road* and *The Dharma Bums*. He wrote numerous books of poetry, approaching the art seriously and passionately. Many of his poetry manuscripts, unable to find a home while he was alive, have been published since his death in 1969.

These books include *The Book of Sketches*, *The Book of Haikus*, the multi-book volume, *Book of Blues, Pomes All Sizes*, and *Scattered Poems,* as well as the contemporaneous volumes, *Heaven and Other Poems,* and *Mexico City Blues*. Some prose works also contain Kerouac poems.

Allen Ginsberg said, "Alas a poet not yet appreciated by the Academy as represented by major college Anthologies used in the quarter century or so since Kerouac's death in 1969" (*Pomes All Sizes* vi).

Is such neglect justified? We know that if a writer produces both poetry and prose, often the poetry will be overlooked - especially if the

74

writer's novels have done well. Few know that Sandra Cisneros began her career as a poet and has published excellent verse volumes with Knopf. Few are familiar with the poetry of the novelist Erica Jong. Master of Fine Arts programs force creative writers to specialize, thus widening the gulf between genres as well as implying that writers can be good only if they are "one note Johnnys".

I have set up a few criteria to my beginning inquiry into the quality of Kerouac's verse:

(1) Willingness to cross taboos to explore dangerous subjects - one form of bravery

(2) Intelligence or awareness

(3) The appearance of vulnerability and honesty - another form of bravery

(4) Original Contributions to the craft

(5) A few magnificent poems

I realize my list is limited and biased, and would be glad to entertain suggestions to improve and enlarge my standards of evaluation if I decide to expand this paper into a book. I will not attempt the impossible: to limit my standards to the purely aesthetic, literary, or technical.

<u>Willingness to Cross Taboos and Explore New Subject Matter:</u>

One function of literature is to bring into the light what festers in darkness. Taboos often get crossed in art. Ginsberg played a role in America's painfully slow but gradual acceptance of homosexuality. Kerouac was confused and ashamed of his gay side. I quote this passage from the 1950s to show Kerouac brave enough to undertake a taboo subject few writers today will explore, childhood sexuality - and perhaps understandably so, with our concern for child abuse. This passage may make you uncomfortable, and we must note that Kerouac may not have seen or recorded all that is happening:

The tall sexual Negro
boy on the junkyard
street near the Gas
Tank Jamaica, about 7
or 8 yrs old, he was
running his palm along
his fly in some Sexual
story to the other little
boy Negro who had his

arm around him as they
came up the street in
the gray rain of Satur-
day afternoon - smoke
emanating from junk fires,
smell of burnt rubber, piles
of tires, junk shops
with old white stoves
on the blackmud sidewalk…
(*Book of Sketches*, 384)

Intelligence and Awareness:

With such a large body of poetic work, I could quote many passages to suggest the intelligence or awareness of this writer. *Mexico City Blues* can be enjoyed for it's shrewdness. Kerouac is not afraid to write abstractly in his poetic work, although he does not do so often. In the passage I am about to quote, abstraction would be hard to avoid:

Light is Late
     yes
          because

it happens after you realize it
     You don't see light
     Until sensation of seeing light
     Is registered in perception. (107)

Vulnerability and Honesty:

The Beat poets Kerouac and Ginsberg were the first confessional poets, before Anne Sexton, John Berryman, Robert Lowell, or Sylvia Plath. Robert Lowell acknowledged his debt to Ginsberg. Here is Kerouac moving from intelligent thought, to immediate observation, to vulnerable self-confession, all in one poem. Poets talk about movement in a poem. This one has it:

That which has not
long to live, frets—
That which lives

forever
 Is full of peace
 And there is no man who'll live forever
 Here it is California,
 little young girls going to
 school in the fresh &
 dewy sidewalks of sleepy
 San Luis....

My life so lonely &
     empty without someone
     to love & lay, & without
     a work to surpass
     myself with, that I
     have nothing nothing
     to write about even
     in the first clear joy
     of morning— (Book of Sketches)

<u>Original Contributions to the Craft</u>:

Kerouac was inspired by California architect and historic preservationist Ed Divine White "to sketch in the streets like a painter but with words." Kerouac's sketching technique reminds one of Zola walking through the tenements of Paris with a notebook, or of Van Gogh getting out of his studio to paint in the fields and streets.

In *The Book of Sketches* Kerouac, with pen and notebook, writes about ships and ship's harbors, people on the streets, rail yards and trains, friends, hitchhiking, and nature. This method creates an immediacy and precision of detail nearly impossible to achieve when in the study, "reflecting in tranquility" - to alter slightly Wordsworth's phrase. At times the details are so overwhelming - or data heavy - that the writing begins to bog down and bore, but at other times sketching is highly effective. Here is one short example, from "Sketch of a Beggar." Recall that this was written in the early 1950s; traditional rhyme and meter were still dominant but have been abandoned by Kerouac:

The strange Allen Ansen-looking
but fat chubby Mexican beggar standing
in front of Woolworth's on Coahuila

behaving spastically, with short haircut
of bangs, brown suitcoat, white shirt,
big pot belly, rocking back and forth
jiggling his hand...He cant conceive that
someone (as I) can be watching from
across *the street 2ⁿᵈ story window...*
(*Book of Sketches* 411*)*

The sketch technique that Kerouac initiated in poetry was acknowledged and borrowed by Allen Ginsberg in such poems as "The Bricklayers' Lunch Hour," and "Iron Horse". Ginsberg carried it forward by using a tape recorder. Kerouac of course knew what he was doing and to ward off criticism wrote the following, short explanation under the title of the book, "Proving that Sketches ain't verse/ But Only What Is."

The sketch is a recording of what is observed, by the senses, in word form, and can make a claim to the truth that verse written from memory may lack, since memory usually is less reliable than perception. I want to quickly mention that Kerouac was also one of the first to experiment with different shapes for poems beyond the traditional acrostics and shape poems. He made list poems, poems with numbered lines, poems with illustrations, and he often moved his lines and stanzas around on a page to give the reader visual variety or to signal pauses.

The second major contribution to the craft of poetry is Kerouac's jazz poetry. He wrote: "I want to be considered a jazz poet blowing a long blues in an afternoon jam session on Sunday...my ideas vary and sometimes roll from chorus to chorus or from halfway through a chorus to halfway through the next" (*Mexico City Blues*). The notion that a theme or idea in a poem does not end with the poem but may play into another poem halfway is unique, as is the emphasis on the oral that most of his "Blues" jazz poetry books maintain. Kerouac's "form" in *Mexico City Blues* was to compose each poem on a small notebook he carried in his pocket.

Such an approach is a new conception of form for literature. Traditionally, form in poetry was determined by metrics, line length syllable counts, or by rhyme scheme. AR Ammons much later modified Kerouac's technique to write a book length poem called "Tape for the Turn of the Year", typing the long skinny poem on a roll of adding machine tape. Ammons' method also relates to *The Dharma Bums* and *On the Road*, where Kerouac used taped sheets so he would not have to pause to insert paper in his typewriter and lose the flow of thought and emotion.

Kerouac also adds, "As in jazz, the form is determined by time, and by the musician's spontaneous phrasing & harmonizing with the beat of time" (*Heaven and other Poems* 56). Kerouac is arguing for an oral-based free verse where the poems develop shape determined by the emotions of moments in time, much like a jazz improviser playing with a tune on stage. This was a time when Columbia University's English department generally disapproved of Whitman. Later, in a letter to Don Allen, his editor at Grove Press, Kerouac would observe, "Funny how they look so old fashioned now, they were written in '54 but now everyone writes like that..." (*Heaven and Other Poems* 58).

My son is a jazz musician, and we sat down one afternoon with Kerouac's 'blues books' and could not find any definite 1950's jazz beats in the lines of those poems. If they follow a beat at all, it is the "beat of time" - the grand time of the universe - not the beat of jazz music performed.

A Few Magnificent Poems:

Innovation in technique distinguished Walt Whitman's verse, but by using that technique Whitman created magnificent poems. A poet only needs a few magnificent poems to make it permanently into the anthologies, and to be more than "a poet's poet," but who can "survive" being compared to Whitman?

Although I believe Kerouac wrote excellent poems using new techniques, he did not succeed magnificently as Whitman does so often, from "Song of Myself" to "Crossing Brooklyn Ferry". Many consider *Mexico City Blues* to be his best poetic work. I do not agree. Such opinion derives from a time when little of Kerouac's verse was available. The choruses of *Mexico City Blues* remind me of Ezra Pound's *Cantos* in their lack of concern for the reader and in the pretentious overuse of names of friends and of Buddhist phrases. They seem closer to the work of John Ashbery than to the work of Beat writers, who wrote about and hoped to be read by the ordinary and even the downtrodden "fellaheen." Still, Kerouac does get off many excellent blues riff poems. I quote from the 242nd chorus:

> *Charley Parker, forgive me—*
> *Forgive me for not answering your eyes—*
> *For not having made any indication*
> *Of that which you can devise—*
> *Charley Parker, pray for me—*
> *Pray for everybody and me*
> *In the Nirvanas of your brain*

Where you hide, indulgent and huge,
No longer Charley Parker
But the secret unswayable name

Where Pound called his individual poems "Cantos," Kerouac calls his "Choruses." The parallel is clear and, like Pound, Kerouac aims to produce an important book length poem sequence. *Mexico City Blues* has long been in print and until a few years ago was a common sight on the poetry shelves of most bookstores. Unlike Pound, Kerouac is able to complete his work and manages to come to a final synthesis and resolution, relating Buddhism to the artist's search for the ultimate, but ultimately choosing the path of art over the path of Buddhism (Nicosia *Memory Babe* 488). The choruses are avant garde in style yet in part religious poems - unusual in our secular era - and that's why Kerouac relates them to jazz on a "Sunday afternoon."

"Touchstones" were the method the Victorian poet and critic Mathew Arnold used to make critical evaluations. Using touchstones means to use other writers as a means of comparison and a way to set up standards. I have used both Whitman and Pound as touchstones to help place Kerouac's achievement as a poet. Comparing Kerouac to Whitman is a bit unfair. Few poets the world over can compete on such a level. Plenty of poets fill the college anthologies who are far from being equals to Whitman.

Does Kerouac deserve to be in the college poetry anthologies as Ginsberg thinks? I firmly believe that Kerouac does, on the strength of poems contained in the recently published *Book of Sketches*. "First Book" has musical lines such as these:

August senses September
In the deeper light of
Its afternoons—senses
Autumn in the brown
burn of the corn, the
stripped tobacco—
the faint singe appearing
on the incomprehensible
horizons... (23)

This sixty-two page, three sectioned poem, achieves not only fine lyric moments, a memorable narrative line, and interesting characters, but also has the immediacy and vivid accuracy of imagery only possible with the sketch technique.

...in the corner where
the light falls flush,
bright creampink
   that shows a tiny
   waving threat of
   spiderweb overlooked

by the greedy house-
keeper...
   (37)

The poem explores the hard life of Kerouac's sister and brother-in-law, living in the South with their child, with compassion and dignity. Here Kerouac does follow Whitman's example to write about the common people in language most can understand. The fact the poem requires little work by scholars or critics will not, I hope, interfere with the poem's future reputation or appreciation.

Kerouac's long poem does not have the dramatic urgency of Ginsberg's great *Kaddish*, but is a fine poem nevertheless with its slower pacing and rhythms. Here the poet speaks with dignity and reserve. There is no sense of the artist's heavy pain or near crackup. Fine moments exist in all of Kerouac's poetic work. *His Book of Haikus* are humorous, readable, and full of wonderful surprise turns of phrase. In his haikus, Kerouac is one of the first to break with the five, seven, five Japanese syllabic pattern imposed on English. The sustained poetic achievements that Kerouac will be remembered for, I believe, are best found in the recently published *Book of Sketches* and *The Book of Haikus*.

From Behind Many Walls
by Alizera Abiz; translated from the Persian by W. N. Herbert

The wail of jackals wakens me

And the futile voice of the dawn

Bugles cough like sick roosters

And the morning sun

Bursts through the needles

Of the garrison's pines

The tired soldier

Hangs his boots around his neck

And pisses in his helmet

Grand Ave. Crossing
by MCD

On 2am strolls down mean street
we watch the cops and robbers
show, and Naked City reruns,
the Kojacks, and Dankos
riding hookers in unmarked cars
while blinded from the head lights
of taxis rolling over John Doe's
head in sand

Never read the statistics nor
catch the 10 o'clock news
with some death and musing
talk on why the crime rates grow
and how to whiten your ragged-ass
clothes before you hide
the heads in sand

Sneak out your padlocked door
before the muggers rise,
or the junkie looks to snatch
his fix by opening the back
of your head you forgot
to hide in sand

So never go out alone at night
just as easy to stay inside
and dial up, or internet,
the pizza delivery guy,
he'll risk his life for your
buck 50 tip before his head
is smashed, writ in blood upon
the sand

My 2am strolls down mean street
darting between the lamps and
taxis, while pimps, like freak show
boulevard barkers' scream
for me to mount their hoes
as I go hide my head in sand

Brother-Souls:

John Clellon Holmes, Jack Kerouac, and the Beat Generation
by Ann Charters and Samuel Charters

Book Review by Michael Hendrick

We recently passed a watershed moment in modern American literature as November, 2012, marked sixty years since John Clellon Holmes introduced the term "Beat Generation" in the New York Times Magazine.

To many, this is the sum of all Holmes is known for.

His seminal Beat novel *Go,* also published sixty years ago (five years ahead of Jack Kerouac's *On the Road),* still remains in the shadow of Kerouac's first book about those times. As evidenced by one of the most popular social networking websites, the cult of celebrity embraces Kerouac. The various tribute pages devoted to Kerouac see traffic from over a quarter of a million people, while the single page dedicated to Holmes draws slightly more than three hundred followers.

Even people who knew him personally seem oblivious to the facts of his life.

In our last issue, Al Hinkle - who is portrayed as a character in both books - noted that Holmes' version of the period "is probably the more accurate." However, Hinkle goes on to speak of Holmes' first wife, "Marian was the love of John's life – he never remarried." The fact is that after divorcing Marian, Holmes married Shirley Radulovich in September, 1953, and the couple remained together until 1988, dying within weeks of each other. Both were victims of cancers attributed to their heavy use of tobacco. These facts are found in the richly informative book *Brother-Souls: John Clellon Holmes, Jack Kerouac, and the Beat Generation* by Ann Charters and Samuel Charters, published in 2010 by the University Press of Mississippi.

Brother-Souls gives us a painstakingly accurate account of the intertwined lives of the two men. In so doing, it also unveils a myriad of previously-unknown facts about peripheral personalities like Hinkle, Allen Ginsberg, William S. Burroughs, Neal Cassady, Herbert Huncke, Gregory Corso, and many others.

If not for the frequently-noted dates and fastidious footnotes, this work of non-fiction would read like a novel – a novel deserving space on the same shelf between *Go* and *On the Road*. While *On the Road* has its hero in the central figure of Cassady as Dean Moriarty, *Go* looks at the same period with its focus on Ginsberg as David Stofsky. It is at Ginberg's party at his apartment in Spanish Harlem where he, Holmes, and Kerouac initially met in July 1948.

Also in our last issue, Ann Charters noted that she and husband Samuel worked on *Brother-Souls* to "redress that wrong" done to Holmes by Kerouac when he portrayed the former as "a wimpy rival." She told us that "It was a difficult book to write but one of its pleasures was the opportunity to give back Holmes his voice as a writer who was an enormous influence on Kerouac."

It can be argued that the first piece of what would become known as Beat Literature appeared in early 1948, when Holmes published his jazz/slang-infused short story, *Tea for Two,* in Jay Landesman's magazine, *Neurotica*. The little magazine founded by St. Louis, Missouri, native Landesman, *Neurotica* became, in style and spirit, the first Beat-themed literary journal, even before the "Beat" term was coined.

A few months earlier, at age twenty-two, he broke into the publishing world with a book review printed in the March, 1948, issue of *Poetry* magazine. The following year, he sent the first chapters of his novel about the colorful characters in the burgeoning bohemian scene, which flourished around him in New York's Greenwich Village, to Landesman.

At roughly the same time, he heard stories about another young writer he referred to as "Karawak" in his journal, who had written a novel, *The Town and The City.* As yet unpublished, the only copy was the fat manuscript, typed by Kerouac, which was being passed around and talked about in the literary circles of New York City's young intellectuals, to which Holmes was privy. Both men met at the party and, after sizing each other up in their perspective journals, soon became fast friends and *confidants.*

Before reaching this point in the book, the Charters' not only detail the childhoods of both men but trace their family trees, as well - on one side back to the 1736 death of Maurice-Louis Alexandre Le Bris de Kerouack, and on the other back to 1594, when George Holmes was born in England. Interestingly, Holmes' family tree included not only one-time presidential candidate John McClellan Holmes, Sr., the celebrated Union general of the Civil War, and the renowned essayist and poet Oliver Wendell Holmes, but also a male ancestor who married a woman from the family Ralph Waldo Emerson was born to.

Ironies and similarities such as their same birthdate of March 12 (Kerouac was five years older) are recounted, as are vivid, shared memories of the Flood of 1936, which Kerouac witnessed from the banks of the Merrimack River in Lowell, Massachusetts. Eighty miles upstream, Holmes watched from the side of the Pemagawassett River, in Plymouth, New Hampshire, as it rose and flowed into the Merrimack, carrying the same waters and debris which neither of them would ever forget.

One early question left open is why they both decided to become writers. The closest thing to an answer may be the "On Spontaneous Prose" section of *The Portable Jack Kerouac*, edited by Ann Charters and published by Viking Penguin in 1995. Significantly, in that volume, she conceived the idea of tracing Kerouac's life through a collection of his writings. When she mentioned the project to Holmes, he told her that he had the same idea in 1965. Not long before his death, Holmes suggested that he and Charters collaborate on it but as his health deteriorated, he passed it back to her with his blessings and an offer of help if she needed it.

In *Brother-Souls*, we have two scribes writing about two other writers. This unique circumstance makes for more than just a diligent study of two convergent writers, it gives insight into their individual writing processes and an insider's look at the business of writing and publishing in America at that time.

Aside from the usual suspects, we meet Landesman and Gershon Legman. Legman would become editor of *Neurotica* and his influence on Holmes is noted. Ginsberg had his first "professional" poem published in the sixth issue of *Neurotica* in 1950. A collaboration written with Kerouac, who took no credit, "Song: Fie My Fum" was met with derision by Legman, who voiced his first impression of the poem by asking, "Did it take two of them to write that piece of shit?" Ginsberg rankled at the fact that Landesman required him to get down on his knees before accepting one of his poems. The poem was four stanzas culled from the poem "Pull My Daisy," to which some accounts credit shared authorship to Cassady, as well.

Carl Solomon, recently released from New York State Psychiatric Institute, where he met Ginsberg, had rented an apartment and as suggested by former institute-roomie Ginsberg, threw a New Year's party to usher in 1950. Landesman showed up with Holmes and was initially attracted by Solomon's "certifiable" state of insanity and his experience with electroshock treatments but, when approached, Solomon steered him towards Ginsberg and Kerouac as being better choices for writers. Just before this scene, we are treated to a look at the meeting of Ginsberg and Solomon, to whom "Howl" was dedicated.

The Charters' follow Ginsberg to his meeting with William Carlos Williams, who advises him to drop rhyming metric poetry in favor of the "variable breath-stop length for metric measurement" as well as looking to his own experiences for the subject matter in his poems.

We see Holmes quickly establish himself as an "accepted" poet by 1950, with submissions published in *Partisan Review* and *Harper's* magazines. However, he felt that the novel was the form he needed to master in order to satisfy himself as being a real writer. To this end, he kept copious journals of the events of his life and of those around him. These were the source material for the chapters of *Go* which he sent Landesman in 1949. Always generous with his friends, Holmes tried to help Ginsberg by sending his poems to his editor at *Partisan Review*. He also spent his time offering encouragement to Kerouac, who was also trying to find his voice in his "road novel" while trying to find a publisher for *The Town and the City*. During 1950-51, while he wrote *Go*, Kerouac visited his apartment daily, to drink, talk, and – most importantly – read the novel page by page as it issued from Holmes' typewriter. It is very likely, given these circumstances, that *On the Road* may never have found a form were it not for the encouragement and example given by the younger Holmes.

While this review/essay is not written to "kneecap" Kerouac, we have to wonder if (after all the ballyhoo, Gap adverts, Facebook pages, and movie treatments) the progression and continued adulation of the Beat Generation as we know it would even have been possible without Holmes. While Ginsberg is typically seen as the gadfly of the collected group of writers, throwing parties and initiating meetings, it was Holmes who opened the doors to *Neurotica* for them. Any writer knows the magnitude of the importance of publishing their first piece of work, outside of school and in a professional publication. Few things are more encouraging than seeing your own name in print for the first time.

To a group of writers who unashamedly pushed the limits of sanity, to whom mental instability actually became a badge of honor, the steep precipice of self-doubt reached by the constant rejection of one's work could be the hardest hurdle to clear. By coincidentally meeting Landesman, Legman, Kerouac, and Ginsberg all in that same July weekend, could Holmes have become the spark that was necessary to set off the Beat firecracker? Perhaps the truest irony of his depiction as "wimpy" is that he is the most obvious catalyst which brought them all exposure.

Neal Cassady is most often seen as the touchstone at the center of the group, although it has been said that they all would have followed Burroughs anywhere he went. The more we unravel Cassady, the less grand of a person he becomes. Holmes mentions the black and blue marks he left on Lu Anne Henderson. His capacity for mental cruelty and abandoning wives and friends at crucial times most likely stem from his own abandonment by his father in Denver, Colorado. Holmes stayed steady in his support of Kerouac's work, even as the latter heralded Cassady as the superior writer in the group and referred to him in a letter as his "only true friend." Cassady responded in kind, in his usual manner, by abandoning him in Mexico City, sick with fever and dysentery.

In his moodiness, Kerouac's misanthropy also got the best of him. Shouting matches between he and Holmes kept to an intellectual level. In barrooms, he was severely beaten more than once, thanks to his mouth and temper but especially as his alcoholic deterioration worsened. Holmes became hesitant to tell him about advances he got from publishers, for fear of setting him off. One point that Kerouac dwelt on during his struggles with *On the Road* was that Holmes "had no right to write a book about everyone's private lives." Both men were doing the same thing, writing about the same people and situations from different angles. Reading *Go* as it was written page by page kept him from duplicating scenes already covered by Holmes - but working around another serious writer could be enervating for anyone.

In all fairness to Kerouac, artists who show genius often do so to express what they cannot in normal life and interpersonal relationships. As artists, writers may plumb themselves to reach those recesses and depths of feeling which are too painful or impossible to relate in any other way. In his essay "Are Writers Born or Made?" he distinguished between talent and genius, noting that many may show "talent" but genius is the rarity. "Geniuses can be scintillating and geniuses can be somber," he noted, "but it's that inescapable sorrowful depth that shines through – originality."

While we appreciate the work they leave behind, the inner torment they endure is not a pretty thing – consider Van Gogh disfiguring himself, Rimbaud cultivating head lice "to throw on passing clergymen," or Artaud's claim to having been "suicided by society." Holmes may have sealed his own fate by being too well-mannered. After all, we learn that Holmes was the only one of Kerouac's friends that his mother Mémère did not dislike.

Nonetheless, about three weeks after Holmes finished the last pages of *Go*, Kerouac became inspired by a letter from Cassady which turned into a rabid series of letters between them. The excitement of these exchanges prompted him to pull all of his notes together and unleash the torrent within upon the now-famous scroll he fed through his typewriter. It seems safe to say that while Cassady sparked him to action, Holmes laid the foundation on those daily visits. The resulting three-week period of speed, coffee, and typing which resulted in *On the Road* has since snowballed into an oft-told tale but *Brother-Souls* reminds the reader that this was not all spontaneous prose. Kerouac's fastidious habit of keeping notebooks provided for a vast amount of his material.

Between the five years from the writing to its publication in 1957, the details and struggles of both men's lives and work come to life in print. Meanwhile, other key events fall into place: Ginsberg meets his life-long companion, Peter Orlovsky, there is the first reading of Ginsberg's poem "Howl for Carl Solomon" at 6 Gallery, Kerouac writes and details the remaining six books of the "Legend of Duluoz" along with three other volumes, the first complete reading of "Howl" takes place (and is attended by Samuel Charters), and the Beat Movement goes mainstream. While most of the key players became victims of the fame, Ginsberg used it to his advantage.

When City Lights got charged with obscenity for distributing *Howl and Other Poems,* more fuel was added to the fire – especially when presiding Judge Clayton W. Horn ruled it to be not obscene. Curiously, Ginsberg slighted Holmes with the omission of his name from the dedication page. Kerouac, Burroughs, and Cassady got a nod from the poet, placing them forever in the highest order of Beats. Holmes had gone out of his way to get Ginsberg published, sending his work to New Directions after his editor at *Partisan Review* passed on it, as well as paying the grand compliment of making him the central character in *Go.* The depiction of Ginsberg in the book posits a good theory as to why he was snubbed. Kerouac had called Holmes "savage" in his treatment of the people he wrote about. Ginsberg, for his part, had been disappointed in the account of his Blakean vision but, at the same time admitted to the veracity of the portrayal of himself.

"You really haven't caught the way it felt," he told Holmes, "but you've caught something else. You've caught the solemn funny little kid I guess I must have been in those days." It seems that no amount of speculation will ever get to the heart of it but the glaring fact of Holmes' exclusion from the dedication and the hurtfulness of the action cannot be overlooked. The Charters' attribute some of it to Holmes distancing himself by leaving New York to live in Old Saybrook, Connecticut, but Cassady and Burroughs were both much further removed geographically.

Six months after the appearance of *On the Road,* Kerouac published *The Subterraneans* (to be followed in another six months by *The Dharma Bums),* heightening his fame but not his luck. With money in his pocket for a change, he traveled out of the United States. As usual, he quickly returned to New York to stay close to his mother. One night, while trying to reach the proper degree of stupor in a local bar, he sustained a broken nose and arm from a beating by a homosexual professional boxer, who claimed he had slurred an insult at him. Later, the depiction of Cassady as pothead led to his arrest and imprisonment.

The whole Beat scene, which thrived in the underground, exploded across the media in 1958, meeting curiosity, admiration, and derision. The term "Beatnik" popped up – a poke in the eye, as it was spawned from the name "Sputnik," the space craft launched by Russia. Nothing linked to Russia could be good in those days. To word irked both men, as they saw it as a symbol of the manipulation, commercialization, and degradation of their once-pure vision. Every critic, pundit, journalist, and magazine writer had something to say about the phenomenon, ranging from suspicions of dangerous revolutions and proliferation of juvenile delinquents to dismissals of idle young hipsters with nothing important to do in life. Holmes had left the United States with Shirley on December 12, 1957, to realize his dream of traveling in Europe for two months, funded by an advance he received for his "jazz" book, *The Horn.*

While working on *Perfect Fools,* his follow-up novel to *Go,* he published a short story which would become *The Horn*'s first chapter in the August, 1953, issue of *Discovery* magazine. The second chapter appeared in *Nugget,* in October 1956. With the rejection *Perfect Fools* by Scribner's, his spirits sank.

He put his energy into writing the "jazz novel," writing the remainder between spring, 1956, and fall of 1957. Although relations between he and Kerouac were deteriorating, Kerouac kept a promise and wrote to a letter praising the novel to Hiram Hayden at Random House two months after the release of *On the Road.*

Accepted immediately and published in July, 1958, it sported a recommendation from Kerouac on the cover. Despite the ongoing "Beat frenzy," sales were moderate, likely due to July traditionally being a slow month for sales or perhaps getting lost among the wave of second-rate, imitation Beat-themed books which flooded the market – potboilers written to cash in on the trend. Selling well enough to require a second printing, mainstream reviews failed to reach the depth of it but it was warmly embraced by the cognoscente, including Studs Terkel and Ralph Gleason. Landesman read it on radio in St. Louis for half an hour, showing how taken he was with it.

Perhaps the most ambitious and meticulously-constructed of all the Beat novels, *The Horn* fascinates, not just by intricacy, but in the marvel of a writer dreaming up such a concept. As for structure, it is the only "true novel" that either he or Kerouac ever produced, not being based on their real-life experiences. In fact, it cannot really be classified as "Beat." As Holmes wrote, regarding the reviews, "The Beat Generation tag has been either ignored (it having nothing to do with the book), or mentioned only in passing, for which I am grateful." Even attempting to describe it presents a daunting task, so here we rely on excerpts from *Brother-Souls,* first with this section from Holmes' journals...

The real origin of the book...lay in my feeling that the jazz artist was the quintessential American artist – that is, that his work hang-ups, his personal neglect by his country, his continual struggle for money, the debasement of his vision by the mean streets, his ofttimes descent into drugs, liquor, and self-destructiveness – all this seemed to me to typify the experience of our great 19th Century American writers: Poe's loneliness, drunkenness and obscurity; Melville's half-of-life anonymity; Hawthorne's hermit years; Emily Dickinson's spinster-bedroom full of immortal poems; Mark Twain's wastage of so much of his talent on get-rich-quick schemes; Whitman's decision to stay with the trolley drivers and whores and good old boys from whom his work took so much sustenance. The novel as it evolved, then, was to be about the American-as-artist.

A month earlier, he explained in a letter:

I was working on three levels at the same time. I wanted each of these characters to represent an American writer, which is the only reason why I put those two little epigraphs in front of each chapter. But I also wanted him to represent a particular kind of jazz musician, and I had to create a fictional character doing these things, so that Edgar Pool, for instance, is Edgar Allen Poe.

Now we give part of the synopsis by Charters/Charters - but note that these are just mere snatches taken from the in-depth explanation they provide, much of what was missed by many initial reviews.

Holmes structured it:

as a kind of dual narrative, each of the narrative streams illustrating and complementing the other. Each of the major characters was introduced in chapters titled "Chorus," and the choruses alternated with chapters titled "Riff," which told the novel's story...Holmes preceded each Chorus with a quotation from one of the nineteenth-century American writers who had given him the novel's theme. With the quotations he was suggesting an identification in each chapter between the jazz musician and the individual writer, and he tied the substance of the quotation as closely as he could to the chapter itself...

The quotation for the first Chorus is from Thoreau, and the name of the musician is Walden Blue. "Walden" is an obvious allusion to Thoreau's Walden *and "Blue" as clearly identifies him as a musician...*

The second Chorus introduces an alto saxophonist named Eddie Wingfield"Wings" Redburn. The quotation is taken from Melville, whose fourth novel was titled Redburn...

A quotation from Hawthorne introduces the Chorus representing the pianist Junious Priest...the musician who was the model for Junius was the avant-garde jazz pianist Thelonious Monk...

The central woman figure...is a singer named "Geordie Dickson," who is locked in a despairing, unending relationship with the novel's main protagonist, the tenor saxophonist Edgar Pool...a combination of singer Billie Holiday and Emily Dickinson...

The name of the trumpeter Curny Finnley is derived from the archetypal figure "Huckelberry Finn," and the Chorus introducing him opens with a quotation from Finn's creator, Mark Twain...Curny Finnley...was in part modeled on trumpeter Dizzy Gillespie...

The Chorus introducing the tenor saxophonist Metro Myland opens with a quotation from Walt Whitman... "Myland" is an allusion to Whitman's personal sense of his Americanism, of the nation as "My land"...Metro, for Holmes, was "just any great big yawping tenor sax player, but he's also Walt Whitman"...

The final two Choruses portray Pool's last hours...from the doomed, desperate Edgar Allen Poe. Holmes' comment on the character of Pool was that his novelistic character was, of course, Lester Young, but also Poe...

As an aid to himself in clarifying the book's structure, Holmes wrote the Choruses first, which described his principal figures. He then wrote the Riffs sections, creating the narrative around his fictitious characters...

Here, it is significant to note that tenor saxophonist/clarinetist Lester Young inspired Ginsberg's creation of "Howl" when the poet wrote several verses in a vocal imitation of Young's chorus-on-chorus jazz progression, the succession of verses building upon each other and raising the rhythmic energy to an ecstatic level. In a 1968 interview with Michael Aldrich, Ginsberg refers to one of the jazz man's signature songs, "Lester Young was what I was thinking about... 'Howl' is all 'Lester Leaps In.'"

The "jazz book" idea provided fodder for many of the vociferous conversations between Holmes and Kerouac. The recognition of its brilliance only grows with time, as will the brilliance of *Brother-Souls*.

In 1958, while Kerouac felt his first anxiety over waiting for royalties from the movie version of *On the Road* (a state of anxiety similarly affected Kerouac fans who waited impatiently until 2012 for its release), Holmes grew increasingly frustrated with the media attention and his realization that the movement they had created ultimately distanced the once close-knit pair. He also bristled at being used as a substitute spokesman for the Beat Generation and the perception of himself as a replacement for Kerouac when the latter could not be found. In spite of this they still kept in touch via letters, proving the true durability of their friendship.

Holmes would face his own problems later that year, in the bleak state of his finances and the emotional turmoil that engulfed him when his father suffered a heart attack in October, forcing an end to years of estrangement. At their home in Old Saybrook, he and Shirley were just about to run out of firewood as the toughest part of the cruel New England winter fell upon them. Luckily, relief came when friends going on vacation asked them to sit their house.

In early February, Landesman sent a hundred dollars in a letter after hearing about their difficulties. These acts of kindness helped them through the winter and in May they were able to return to visit New York when Landesman staged the first and only Beat musical, "The Nervous Set," and all performances sold-out. Kerouac showed up at the theater drunk and promptly fell asleep in his seat, vanishing during the intermission. The trip gave them some respite but in July a rush-hour accident on the New Jersey Turnpike put his father back in the hospital in Camden and one of his hands had to be amputated as a result. In the days that followed, a stroke paralyzed half of his father's body.

Weeks spent keeping vigil at the bedside, trying to help nurse his father back to health led to exhaustion and near the end of August, John McClellan Holmes Sr., after weeks of suffering and staring at the stump of his hand, lost the will to live and passed away.

Although their relationship was frequently antagonistic, the event haunted the junior Holmes (who had taken "Clellon" as a pen-name to allay confusion with the well-known poet, John Holmes) for years. He wrote about the experience in the poem "Too-Late Words for My Father," which he completed years later, in 1973. Old friend Alan Harrington, novelist and *On the Road* character, helped him with the hospital expenses. The chronic emotional devastation left him unable to write much outside of his journals and he slipped into one of the most unproductive periods of his life. Days spent drinking and arguing with Shirley exacerbated the situation. An unpaid electric bill for eight dollars forced him to hide upstairs when the electric company worker came to shut off his power in September of 1961 and the following month he was arrested for shoplifting a few dollars worth of groceries at a local market and the local press used the story to lampoon him with an embarrassing, supposedly-funny headline.

At this point something snapped inside him. A lesser man may have acted out against himself but in Holmes' case, the situation forced him to pull himself together, deal with his creative block and begin writing again.

As is often the case, a great man finds his true measure at the worst of times, not the best. It is also notable that through it all, Shirley stayed with him, working where she could to support them both. Holmes appears to have been one of the few of his peers to maintain a traditional "'til death do we part" relationship, one of life's true treasures.

His turn back to the positive side spurred an equally positive reaction from magazines he submitted his work to, after braving it through a short period of rejected stories. Around the time he came to terms with the fact that his novels would never bring him as much fame as his poetry and non-fiction, he won *Playboy* magazine's Best Non-Fiction award for 1964, with the essay, "Revolution Below the Belt." This shows how deeply Legman had influenced him with his fixation on all things sexual years earlier.

His sister Liz, also a writer, made the acquaintance of Nelson Algren, author of the groundbreaking novels, *A Walk on the Wild Side* and *The Man with the Golden Arm*. During this period of regeneration, she introduced the pair. Once again, he enjoyed the luxury of intellectual stimulation that is peculiar to like-minded writers. For his part, Algren equally valued conversation with a mind sharp enough to write a book like *The Horn*.

Although he appeared the stronger of the two "brothers," Kerouac never found his feet once he started balancing them on bottles. The sad facts of his self-immolation fill pages and support a variation on one of Legman's favorite themes – that violence in modern society results directly from the repression of our sexuality. In his case, the violence turned inward and bespeaks the result of not being able to fully love a woman in a true manner. Sex is more than just a function of the genitalia. It is an outward expression of love and tenderness. He loved his mother, there is no doubting that, but his inability to correlate love and sex (the Cassadian logic of all people being apples and we just need to pick them and eat them as we will) may have been his undoing. This is not something Ann and Samuel Charters broach in the book but this writer's attempt at explaining his trip from top of the heap to bottom of the glass.

Although we suggest that Holmes sparked the kindling that lit the Beat fire, it is commonly accepted that Kerouac is responsible for the Beat Movement gaining the momentum to be a worldwide cultural revolution, these sixty years later. He is the primary visual symbol. He is the face of it today, not the angelic hipster Cassady, whose death from exposure in the Mexican night froze "blood on the tracks" after he bridged the generation gap between Beat and Hippie; not even Ginsberg who may have been the most prolific producer of the lot. His radicalism and homosexuality may have been off-putting to a straight society.

Kerouac - the older brother who died as the younger, the televised, the Adonis – he is the symbol who put a face on the new culture, at the piano with Steve Allen speaking cool and hip and mellifluous.

The triumph of Holmes' later years overshadow the misery of those when he was beaten-down Beat, in the truest sense of the word. The world of academia sought him out and he accepted residencies at several fine schools. Never giving up on the novel, he produced two more, *Get Home Free* in 1964 and *Nothing More to Declare in 1967*. More books appeared posthumously. He enjoyed the company of his old cronies when Ginsberg brought them together at Naropa Institute for a celebration of Kerouac's work on the twenty-fifth anniversary of the publication on *On the Road* in 1982. His dedication to his craft supplied him with purpose and a way to communicate while fighting a recurrent cancer when it robbed his frantic gift of speech.

He survived nineteen years after Kerouac and twenty after Cassady. In March, 1988, he died at age sixty-two, beloved wife Shirley with him as ever. In death, as in life, she followed him just two weeks later, a common fate of couples who share a true love. Earlier in the year, he learned that three of his novels would soon be reprinted on Thunder Mouth Press, so with his once-greatest fear of vanishing "without leaving some trace" vanquished, this surely gave him strength as mortality fleeted.

To paraphrase Kerouac's paraphrasing in "Are Writers Born or Made?" - *It ain't whatcha live, it's the way atcha live it.*

This reviewer hopes the reader bears in mind that this piece may seem full of facts but it is only a fraction, less than even a fiftieth, of pages presented in *Brother-Souls*. In the entire canon of Beat books, it is arguably the single, most comprehensive view of the scene as it unfolded - and absolutely the most authoritative work on Holmes and Kerouac. It is the only book which comes to mind where the footnote pages themselves are a treat to read.

We come away from reading it with the feeling of just completing a course in history, absorbing enough to get an A+ on the subject. If some obvious facts are missing here, it is simply because we chose to focus primarily on Holmes, then Kerouac and the others.

We first became aware of Ann Charters in 1973, when her biography on Kerouac (with Samuel) became widely celebrated and instantly considered as the definitive book on him. While relishing the blues of Lightnin' Hopkins since the 1970s and growing up with the music of Country Joe and the Fish even earlier on life's soundtrack, we only recently discovered our ignorance of the fact that Samuel Charters had a hand in delivering these important sounds. A Grammy Award winner, he produced five of the six Country Joe LPs. In 1959, he found Hopkins in Houston, Texas, and did field recordings of him. These were released on the Folkways label and led to a rediscovery by an appreciative new audience

At last count, eighteen books credit him as author. That is aside from collaborations listed in the thirty-book bibliography of Ann Charters, printed in our last issue. This count does not include *Portents*, the self-published small-press they ran in the 1960s. In literature and music the couple are a national treasure, both gifted individually and as a team. She is also an accomplished, recorded ragtime pianist. A recently-posted Youtube video (you can find it on www.beatdom.com) shows them working together, reading poetry at a Beat event in England earlier this year.

Ann Charters and Samuel Charters did more than write a large part of *Brother-Souls*, they lived it and witnessed it first-hand.

Buy it!

All images are reprinted courtesy University Press of Mississippi. Page 86, John, Provincetown, Massachusetts, 1949, courtesy John Clellon Holmes; Page 89, John on the back steps, Old Saybrook, 1981. Photo: Ann Charters; Page 91, The Horn, 1958; Page 95, At Kerouac's graveside, Lowell, Massachusetts, John Clellon Holmes, Allen Ginsberg, Gregory Corso, October 24, 1969. Photo: Ann Charters.

American Zen

by Philip Rafferty

Zen Buddhism is nearly impossible to write about. The use of words and logic to explain Zen are in opposition to its nature, one free of such restrictions. The question then arises: how can we know the principles of Zen if we can't directly talk about them? The solution is that we study the principals of Zen, which are contrivances, to forget them in order to move closer to Zen. The point of such a contradictory exercise is to provide a base from which we practice zazen[1] in order to shed away our dualistic ways of thought and proceed towards Satori[2], or Zen enlightenment. This is at the core of the Zen Buddhist practice and was central to the Buddhist influenced work of the Beat Generation writers Allen Ginsberg, Gary Snyder, and Jackson Mac Low. These writers used Zen Buddhism as an influence to present a countercultural Zen aesthetic that frees the reader from the mainstream materialistic culture by exemplifying what an understanding of a truer

---

1   1. *Zazen* is the Buddhist meditative practice of "opening the hand of thought." This is done while sitting and allowing the mind to become unhindered by its many layers. When this is achieved the experience gives way to an insight into the nature of existence and the individual then gains satori or enlightenment.

2   2. *Satori* refers to the "enlightenment" or individual awakening to a world that transcends the dualistic mind and deeply realizes the nature of existence as it is achieved through Zen.

nature of existence or satori-like experience might look like with poems that mirror the meditative practice of zazen. Ginsberg's "Last Night in Calcutta" synthesizes Zen enlightenment while Snyder's "Riprap" and Mac Low's "1st Dance—Making Things New—6 February 1964" provide us with zazen meditative "kôans" to contemplate. These poems are awakenings that transcend the dualistic and show us how we can arrive at a deeply realized nature of existence.

Allen Ginsberg's "Last Night In Calcutta" begins: "Still night./ The old Clock ticks,/ half past two. A ringing of crickets/ awake in the ceiling. The gate is locked/on the street outside--sleepers, mustaches,/nakedness,/but no desire. A few mosquitoes/waken the itch, the fan turns slowly--/a car thunders along the black asphalt,/a bull snorts, something is expected--/Time sits solid in the four yellow walls." (1-11) The opening phrase "Still night" frames the poem and the quietude of this opening utterance accomplishes two things: it centers the poem in the present, and invites us into Ginsberg's zazen meditation. The lines that follow further establish this work as a meditation. The poet's perception of his surrounding, the "old clock ticks…a ringing of crickets/ awake in the ceiling," show him embarking on his meditation and exemplify his opening of "the hand of thought" through zazen practice. These lines are fixed in Calcutta, May 22, 1963, and present a grounded immediacy. This is what is, there is no construction, no imposition, these lines are and "time sits solid in the four yellow walls" of this place.

This opening initiates the zazen meditation and becomes more deeply entranced in Zen with the twelfth and thirteenth lines that read, "No one is here, emptiness filled with train/ whistles & dog barks, answered a block away." (12-13) The statement is curious. If no one is here, who is writing the poem? The disintegration of the ego, of "I", is essential in Zen, and for man to move closer to satori he must not suffer under the imposition of selfhood. Ginsberg is exercising this freedom, removing signs of egotism and self in order to get to the true nature of existence. We must note that Ginsberg, quite a self referential, does not use any personal pronouns in this poem and this is a testament to this poem's Zen aesthetic. These selfless lines drive the poem deeper into zazen and set the poem in orbit around a possible satori state of transcendence.

The rest of the poem hovers around the Zen principal of satori and shows what this awakening to the nature of existence might look like. Ginsberg shows us that his meditation reshapes his understanding of existence and delivers him to a higher understanding through Zen. This epiphany is exemplified in the thirty-sixth line of the poem: "Skin is sufficient to be skin, that is all." The realization that skin is skin shows the new way of thought achievable through enlightenment. This line is a shedding of meaning and focuses on the true nature of existence through Zen as being one that is inexplicable. This poem encapsulates Ginsberg's aesthetic understanding of Zen and its poetic application. Ginsberg simulates the zazen process for us as readers with this poem and shows us what a satori epiphany looks like.

Gary Snyder's poem "Riprap" and Jackson Mac Low's "1st Dance—Making Things New—6 February 1964" are both Zen poems that provide us with "riprap" of our own on our journey towards satori. Snyder's and Mac Low's poems are not exhibitions of satori or an awakened state (as we saw with Ginsberg's "Last Night in Calcutta") but instead they are kôans that are meant to provide us with meditations that contribute to our Zen practice. We must quickly define "Kôan" and "Riprap" so that we may understand how these poets use these ideas in their poems. A "kôan" is a fundamental part of Zen Buddhism; it is a story, dialogue, question, or statement provided by a Zen master for a student to meditate on during zazen. A kôan is meant to transcend rational thought moving one closer to an intuitive state on the way to satori. "Riprap" is loosely defined as a set of stones one lies down on as a path to create traction, and we can see how a kôan might be considered a mental riprap of sorts. The concept of both of these poems, as kôans that provide us as readers with riprap, creates a framework into which we may understand the Zen aesthetic Mac Low and Snyder employ.

Snyder's poem "Riprap" opens with the lines, "Lay down these words/ before your mind like rocks." (1-2) This is an invitation. The poem is presented as a kôan with these lines, and Snyder is asking us to use this poem as "riprap" for our own personal zazen exercise. Snyder, like a Zen master, guides us through a meditation: "place [these words] solid, by hands/ in choice of place, set before the body of the mind in space and time:" (3-6) This instruction ends with a colon and the poem then lists what we are to "set before the body of the mind" to meditate on in this kôan. Snyder lists, "Solidity of bark, lead, or wall/ riprap of things:/ Cobble of milky way,/ straying planets/ these poems, people." (7-11) The solidities in the first line send us into contemplation on the categorization of things and attempts to strip the meaning from this duality through juxtaposition. We are challenged to question this quality of things as "solid." The list of "milky way" "straying planets" "poems" and "people" presents another set of comparisons. Snyder's kôan poem induces a zazen state that forces us question the linguistic duality or separation of things, and we can't help but meditate on the question: are we part of the Milky Way, a straying planet, a person, or are we poems? Finishing this poem we come to question the initial invitation of "laying down these words" and sit with the kôan contemplating if these words are riprap from which we gain a footing on our Zen way, or are we meant to lie down and forget the words that make us this poem.

Jackson Mac Low's "1st Dance—Making Things New—6 February 1964" is a kôan that invites us into contemplation like the poem "Riprap" by Gary Snyder. The fundamental difference between Snyder's poem and Mac Low's is that "1st Dance" is more obtuse and lacks the instructive quality seen in Snyder's poem. "1st Dance", from the collection *The Pronouns,* opens with the pronoun "He."(1) This is quite different from Ginsberg's pronounless "Last Night in Calcutta" and Snyder's use of the possessive "your" in "Riprap." Mac Low's use of the indefinite pronoun creates an ambiguity not present in the other poems. We immediately begin to question who "He" is. The poem then proceeds with a series of surrealistic images of what "He" does. The first two lines read, "He makes himself comfortable/ & matches parcels." What does Mac Low mean by "matches parcels?" There is an inherent contradiction in "matching" or bringing together in pairs and "parceling" or dividing into portions. The lines that follow also stultify. Mac Low writes in lines 6-7, "Soon after, he's giving cushions or seeming to do so,/ taking opinions" and we are left to wonder what this means. These lines act, just as Snyder's poem, as a kôan, but are more perplexing because

of these strange images that clear our mind and break down our categorized thought.

Mac Low ends the poem with, "A little while later he gets out with things/ & finally either rewards someone for something or goes up under/ something." (15-17) and these final lines are an ambiguous riddle which sends us into a state of zazen that transcends rational thought. There is less invitation and instruction here compared with Snyder's "Riprap" and Mac Low seems less of a Zen master and more of a Zen practitioner. Mac Low pushes with this poem towards the transcendence of dualistic meaning and both ushers us and forces himself along on the journey towards satori. This poem offers a pure Zen aesthetic that initially confounds but hidden deep within it is the possibility of eventual satori state of enlightenment.

There are a few problems regarding these poems as Zen poems that we must confront. Zen Buddhism is a laborious task. There are no quick roads in Zen. In the early 1950s, D.T. Suzuki and Alan Watts popularized the principles of Zen in the Western world, and made them seem quickly accessible to all and any, (these poets are adapting Zen from what they learned from Watts and Suzuki and these poems make Zen seem extremely accessible). This claim for Zen as accessible to all is not the case. Zen is something you dedicate your life to, that you must practice rigorously each day. Zazen is an especially painstaking activity of thousands of hours of meditation in order that one might come close to satori, while knowing quite well that they might never achieve this understanding. If this is the case, why do Ginsberg, Snyder and Mac Low write these poems that synthesize the zazen meditation? The answer is that these poets are showing us how this Zen process works and are using the zazen meditation and the kôan as a framework to present a poetic counter-reality that uses Buddhism as an aesthetic principal. This type of poem allows Ginsberg to show us what satori might look like, and for Snyder and Mac Low to help us on our way by providing meditative kôans. These poems invite the reader into a zazen state that opens his eyes to question: how can we transcend rational thought, break free of mainstream materialistic culture, and get closer to understanding the true nature of existence? These men show us this is possible, and that the Zen way is the road that will get us there even if it is not true to the sense of Zen, but instead what we then must call "American Zen."

*

Photo: Zen garden, South Korea, by David S. Wills

ALAN W. WATTS

Beat Zen
quare Zen
and ZEN

Jackson Mac Low

♠

Thing of
Beauty

♥

New and Selected Works

Edited by Anne Tardos

ALLEN
GINSBER
SELECTED POE
1947–1995

ck Kerou

SELECTED WRITINGS OF D. T. SUZUKI

ZEN
BUDDHISM

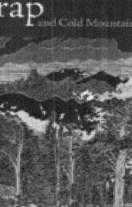

anniversary edi

Gary Sny
prap and Cold Mountain

21196107R00055

Made in the USA
Lexington, KY
03 March 2013